THE BOSS AND THE MACHINE

ROOSEVELT EDITION

∴

VOLUME 43
THE CHRONICLES
OF AMERICA SERIES
ALLEN JOHNSON
EDITOR

GERHARD R. LOMER
CHARLES W. JEFFERYS
ASSISTANT EDITORS

"LET US PREY"

After the cartoon by Thomas Nast

THE BOSS
AND THE MACHINE

A CHRONICLE OF THE POLITICIANS
AND PARTY ORGANIZATION
BY SAMUEL P. ORTH

NEW HAVEN: YALE UNIVERSITY PRESS
TORONTO: GLASGOW, BROOK & CO.
LONDON: HUMPHREY MILFORD
OXFORD UNIVERSITY PRESS
1921

Copyright, 1919, by Yale University Press

CONTENTS

ILLUSTRATION

THE BOSS AND THE MACHINE

∴

CHAPTER I

THE RISE OF THE PARTY

THE party system is an essential instrument of Democracy. Wherever government rests upon the popular will, there the party is the organ of expression and the agency of the ultimate power. The party is, moreover, a forerunner of Democracy, for parties have everywhere preceded free government. Long before Democracy as now understood was anywhere established, long before the American colonies became the United States, England was divided between Tory and Whig. And it was only after centuries of bitter political strife, during which a change of ministry would not infrequently be accompanied by bloodshed or voluntary exile, that England finally emerged with a government deriving its powers from the consent of the governed.

The functions of the party, both as a forerunner and as a necessary organ of Democracy, are well exemplified in American experience. Before the Revolution, Tory and Whig were party names used in the colonies to designate in a rough way two ideals of political doctrine. The Tories believed in the supremacy of the Executive, or the King; the Whigs in the supremacy of Parliament. The Tories, by their rigorous and ruthless acts giving effect to the will of an un-English King, soon drove the Whigs in the colonies to revolt, and by the time of the Stamp Act (1765) a well-knit party of colonial patriots was organized through committees of correspondence and under the stimulus of local clubs called "Sons of Liberty." Within a few years, these patriots became the Revolutionists, and the Tories became the Loyalists. As always happens in a successful revolution, the party of opposition vanished, and when the peace of 1783 finally put the stamp of reality upon the Declaration of 1776, the patriot party had won its cause and had served its day.

Immediately thereafter a new issue, and a very significant one, began to divide the thought of the people. The Articles of Confederation, adopted as a form of government by the States during a lull in the nationalistic fervor, had utterly failed to perform the functions of a national government. Financially the Confederation was a beggar at the doors of the States; commercially it was impotent; politically it was bankrupt. The new issue was the formation of a national government that should in reality represent a federal nation, not a collection of touchy States. Washington in his farewell letter to the American people at the close of the war (1783) urged four considerations: a strong central government, the payment of the national debt, a well-organized militia, and the surrender by each State of certain local privileges for the good of the whole. His "legacy," as this letter came to be called, thus bequeathed to us Nationalism, fortified on the one hand by Honor and on the other by Preparedness.

The Confederation floundered in the slough of inadequacy for several years, however, before the people were sufficiently impressed with the necessity of a federal government. When, finally, through the adroit maneuver of Alexander Hamilton and James Madison, the Constitutional Convention was called in 1787, the people were in a somewhat chastened mood, and delegates were sent to the Convention from all the States except Rhode Island.

No sooner had the delegates convened and chosen George Washington as presiding officer, than the two opposing sides of opinion were revealed, the nationalist and the particularist, represented by the Federalists and the Anti-Federalists, as they later termed themselves. The Convention, however, was formed of the conservative leaders of the States, and its completed work contained in a large measure, in spite of the great compromises, the ideas of the Federalists. This achievement was made possible by the absence from the Convention of the two types of men who were to prove the greatest enemy of the new document when it was presented for popular approval, namely, the office-holder or politician, who feared that the establishment of a central government would deprive him of his influence, and the popular demagogue, who viewed with suspicion all evidence of organized authority. It was these two types, joined by a third — the conscientious objector — who formed the Anti-Federalist party to oppose the adoption of the new Constitution. Had this opposition been well organized, it could unquestionably have defeated the Constitution, even against its brilliant protagonists, Hamilton, Madison, Jay, and a score of other masterly men.

The unanimous choice of Washington for President gave the new Government a non-partizan initiation. In every way Washington attempted to foster the spirit of an undivided household. He warned his countrymen against partizanship and sinister political societies. But he called around his council board talents which represented incompatible ideals of government. Thomas Jefferson, the first Secretary of State, and Alexander Hamilton, the first Secretary of the Treasury, might for a time unite their energies under the wise chieftainship of Washington, but their political principles could never be merged. And when, finally, Jefferson resigned, he became forthwith the leader of the opposition — not to Washington, but to Federalism as interpreted by Hamilton, John Adams, and Jay.

The name Anti-Federalist lost its aptness after the inauguration of the Government. Jefferson and his school were not opposed to a federal government. They were opposed only to its pretensions, to its assumption of centralized power.

Jefferson-Demo-Repub - opposite to strong central
power of Federalists (Adams
Hamilt'

6   THE BOSS AND THE MACHINE

Their deep faith in popular control is revealed in
the name they assumed, Democratic-Republican.
They were eager to limit the federal power to the
glorification of the States; the Federalists were
ambitious to expand the federal power at the
expense of localism.   This is what Jefferson meant
when he wrote to Washington as early as 1792,
"The Republican party wish to preserve the
Government in its present form."   Now this is
a very definite and fundamental distinction.   It
involves the political difference between government by the people and government by the
representatives of the people, and the practical
difference between a government by law and a
government by mass-meeting.

Jefferson was a master organizer.   At letter-
writing, the one means of communication in those
days, he was a Hercules.   His pen never wearied.
He soon had a compact party.   It included not
only most of the Anti-Federalists, but the small
politicians, the tradesmen and artisans, who had
worked themselves into a ridiculous frenzy over the
French Revolution and who despised Washington
for his noble neutrality.   But more than these, Jefferson won over a number of distinguished men who
had worked for the adoption of the Constitution,

the ablest of whom was James Madison, often called "the Father of the Constitution."

The Jeffersonians, thus representing largely the debtor and farmer class, led by men of conspicuous abilities, proceeded to batter down the prestige of the Federalists. They declared themselves opposed to large expenditures of public funds, to eager exploitation of government ventures, to the Bank, and to the Navy, which they termed "the great beast with the great belly." The Federalists included the commercial and creditor class and that fine element in American life composed of leading families with whom domination was an instinct, all led, fortunately, by a few idealists of rare intellectual attainments. And, with the political stupidity often characteristic of their class, they stumbled from blunder to blunder. In 1800 Thomas Jefferson, who adroitly coined the mistakes of his opponents into political currency for himself, was elected President. He had received no more electoral votes than Aaron Burr, that mysterious character in our early politics, but the election was decided by the House of Representatives, where, after seven days' balloting, several Federalists, choosing what to them was the lesser of two evils, cast the deciding votes for Jefferson.

When the Jeffersonians came to power, they
no longer opposed federal pretensions; they now,
by one of those strange veerings often found in
American politics, began to give a liberal interpretation to the Constitution, while the Federalists with equal inconsistency became strict
constructionists. Even Jefferson was ready to
sacrifice his theory of strict construction in order
to acquire the province of Louisiana.

The Jeffersonians now made several concessions
to the manufacturers, and with their support
linked to that of the agriculturists Jeffersonian
democracy flourished without any potent opposition. The second war with England lent it a
doubtful luster but the years immediately following the war restored public confidence. Trade
flourished on the sea. The frontier was rapidly
pushed to the Mississippi and beyond into the
vast empire which Jefferson had purchased. When
everyone is busy, no one cares for political
issues, especially those based upon philosophical
differences. So Madison and Monroe succeeded
to the political regency which is known as the
Virginia Dynasty.

This complacent epoch culminated in Monroe's
"Era of Good Feeling," which proved to be

only the hush before the tornado. The election of 1824 was indecisive, and the House of Representatives was for a second time called upon to decide the national choice. The candidates were John Quincy Adams, Andrew Jackson, Henry Clay, and William H. Crawford. Clay threw his votes to Adams, who was elected, thereby arousing the wrath of Jackson and of the stalwart and irreconcilable frontiersmen who hailed him as their leader. The Adams term merely marked a transition from the old order to the new, from Jeffersonian to Jacksonian democracy. Then was the word Republican dropped from the party name, and Democrat became an appellation of definite and practical significance.

By this time many of the older States had removed the early restrictions upon voting, and the new States carved out of the West had written manhood suffrage into their constitutions. This new democracy flocked to its imperator; and Jackson entered his capital in triumph, followed by a motley crowd of frontiersmen in coonskin caps, farmers in butternut-dyed homespun, and hungry henchmen eager for the spoils. For Jackson had let it be known that he considered his election a mandate by the people to fill the offices with his political adherents.

So the Democrats began their new lease of life with an orgy of spoils. "Anybody is good enough for any job" was the favorite watchword. But underneath this turmoil of desire for office, significant party differences were shaping themselves. Henry Clay, the alluring orator and master of compromise, brought together a coalition of opposing fragments. He and his following objected to Jackson's assumption of vast executive prerogatives, and in a brilliant speech in the Senate Clay espoused the name Whig. Having explained the origin of the term in English and colonial politics, he cried: "And what is the present but the same contest in another form? The partizans of the present Executive sustain his favor in the most boundless extent. The Whigs are opposing executive encroachment and a most alarming extension of executive power and prerogative. They are contending for the rights of the people, for free institutions, for the supremacy of the Constitution and the laws."

There soon appeared three practical issues which forced the new alignment. The first was the Bank. The charter of the United States

Bank was about to expire, and its friends sought a renewal. Jackson believed the Bank an enemy of the Republic, as its officers were anti-Jacksonians, and he promptly vetoed the bill extending the charter. The second issue was the tariff. Protection was not new; but Clay adroitly renamed it, calling it "the American system." It was popular in the manufacturing towns and in portions of the agricultural communities, but was bitterly opposed by the slave-owning States. A third issue dealt with internal improvements. All parts of the country were feeling the need of better means of communication, especially between the West and the East. Canals and turnpikes were projected in every direction. Clay, whose imagination was fervid, advocated a vast system of canals and roads financed by national aid. But the doctrine of states-rights answered that the Federal Government had no power to enter a State, even to spend money on improvements, without the consent of that State. And, at all events, for Clay to espouse was for Jackson to oppose.

These were the more important immediate issues of the conflict between Clay's Whigs and Jackson's Democrats, though it must be acknowledged that the personalities of the leaders were quite as much an issue as any of the policies which they espoused. The Whigs, however, proved unequal to the task of unhorsing their foes; and, with two exceptions, the Democrats elected every President from Jackson to Lincoln. The exceptions were William Henry Harrison and Zachary Taylor, both of whom were elected on their war records and both of whom died soon after their inauguration. Tyler, who as Vice-President succeeded General Harrison, soon estranged the Whigs, so that the Democratic triumph was in effect continuous over a period of thirty years.

Meanwhile, however, another issue was shaping the destiny of parties and of the nation. It was an issue that politicians dodged and candidates evaded, that all parties avoided, that publicists feared, and that presidents and congressmen tried to hide under the tenuous fabric of their compromises. But it was an issue that persisted in keeping alive and that would not down, for it was an issue between right and wrong. Three times the great Clay maneuvered to outflank his opponents over the smoldering fires of the slavery issue, but he died before the repeal of the Missouri Compromise gave the death-blow to his loosely gathered coalition. Webster, too, and Calhoun, the other members of that brilliant trinity which represented the genius of Constitutional Unionism, of States-Rights, and of Conciliation, passed away before the issue was squarely faced by a new party organized for the purpose of opposing the further expansion of slavery.

This new organization, the Republican party, rapidly assumed form and solidarity. It was composed of Northern Whigs, of anti-slavery Democrats, and of members of several minor groups, such as the Know-Nothing or American party, the Liberty party, and included as well some of the despised Abolitionists. The vote for Frémont, its first presidential candidate, in 1856, showed it to be a sectional party, confined to the North. But the definite recognition of slavery as an issue by an opposition party had a profound effect upon the Democrats. Their Southern wing now promptly assumed an uncompromising attitude, which, in 1860, split the party into factions. The Southern wing named Breckinridge; the Northern wing named Stephen A. Douglas; while many Democrats as well as Whigs took refuge in a third party, calling itself the Constitutional Union, which named John Bell. This division cost the Democrats the election, for, under the unique and inspiring leadership of Abraham Lincoln, the Republicans rallied the anti-slavery forces of the North and won.

Slavery not only racked the parties and caused new alignments; it racked and split the Union. It is one of the remarkable phenomena of our political history that the Civil War did not destroy the Democratic party, though the Southern chieftains of that party utterly lost their cause. The reason is that the party never was as purely a Southern as the Republican was a Northern party. Moreover, the arrogance and blunders of the Republican leaders during the days of Reconstruction helped to keep it alive. A baneful political heritage has been handed down to us from the Civil War — the solid South. It overturns the national balance of parties, perpetuates a pernicious sectionalism, and deprives the South of that bipartizan rivalry which keeps open the currents of political life.

Since the Civil War the struggle between the two dominant parties has been largely a struggle between the Ins and the Outs. The issues that have divided them have been more apparent than real. The tariff, the civil service, the trusts, and the long list of other "issues" do not denote fundamental differences, but only variations of degree. Never in any election during this long interval has there been definitely at stake a great national principle, save for the currency issue of 1896 and the colonial question following the War with Spain. The revolt of the Progressives in 1912 had a character of its own; but neither of the old parties squarely joined issue with the Progressives in the contest which followed. The presidential campaign of 1916 afforded an opportunity to place on trial before the people a great cause, for there undoubtedly existed then in the country two great and opposing sides of public opinion — one for and the other against war with Germany. Here again, however, the issue was not joined but was adroitly evaded by both the candidates.

None the less there has been a difference between the two great parties. The Republican party has been avowedly nationalistic, imperialistic, and in favor of a vigorous constructive foreign policy. The Democratic party has generally accepted the lukewarm international policy of Jefferson and the

exaltation of the locality and the plain individual
as championed by Jackson. Thus, though in a
somewhat intangible and variable form, the doc-
trinal distinctions between Hamilton and Jefferson
have survived.

In the emergence of new issues, new parties
are born. But it is one of the singular char-
acteristics of the American party system that
third parties are abortive. Their adherents serve
mainly as evangelists, crying their social and
economic gospel in the political wilderness. If
the issues are vital, they are gradually absorbed
by the older parties.

Before the Civil War several sporadic parties
were formed. The most unique was the Anti-
Masonic party. It flourished on the hysteria
caused by the abduction of William Morgan of
Batavia, in western New York, in 1826. Morgan
had written a book purporting to lay bare
the secrets of Freemasonry. His mysterious dis-
appearance was laid at the doors of leading
Freemasons; and it was alleged that members of
this order placed their secret obligations above
their duties as citizens and were hence unfit for
public office. The movement became impressive
in Pennsylvania, Vermont, Massachusetts, Ohio,

and New York. It served to introduce Seward and Fillmore into politics. Even a national party was organized, and William Wirt, of Maryland, a distinguished lawyer, was nominated for President. He received, however, only the electoral votes of Vermont. The excitement soon cooled, and the party disappeared.

The American or Know-Nothing party had for its slogan "America for Americans," and was a considerable factor in certain localities, especially in New York and the Middle States, from 1853 to 1856. The Free Soil party, espousing the cause of slavery restriction, named Martin Van Buren as its presidential candidate and polled enough votes in the election of 1848 to defeat Cass, the Democratic candidate. It did not survive the election of 1852, but its essential principle was adopted by the Republican party.

Since the Civil War, the currency question has twice given life to third-party movements. The Greenbacks of 1876–1884 and the Populists of the 90's were both of the West. Both carried on for a few years a vigorous crusade, and both were absorbed by the older parties as the currency question assumed concrete form and became a commanding political issue. Since 1872, the

2

Prohibitionists have named national tickets.
Their question, which was always dodged by the
dominant parties, is now rapidly nearing a solution.

The one apparently unreconcilable element in
our political life is the socialistic or labor party.
Never of great importance in any national election, the various labor parties have been of considerable influence in local politics. Because of
its magnitude, the labor vote has always been
courted by Democrats and Republicans with equal
ardor but with varying success.

CHAPTER II

THE RISE OF THE MACHINE

IDEAS or principles alone, however eloquently and insistently proclaimed, will not make a party. There must be organization. Thus we have two distinct practical phases of American party politics: one regards the party as an agency of the electorate, a necessary organ of democracy; the other, the party as an organization, an army determined to achieve certain conquests. Every party has, therefore, two aspects, each attracting a different kind of person: one kind allured by the principles espoused; the other, by the opportunities of place and personal gain in the organization. The one kind typifies the body of voters; the other the dominant minority of the party.

When one speaks, then, of a party in America, he embraces in that term: first, the tenets or platform for which the party assumes to stand (i.e., principles that may have been wrought out of experience, may have been created by public opinion, or were perhaps merely made out of hand by manipulators); secondly, the voters who profess attachment to these principles; and thirdly, the political expert, the politician with his organization or machine. Between the expert and the great following are many gradations of party activity, from the occasional volunteer to the chieftain who devotes all his time to "politics."

It was discovered very early in American experience that without organization issues would disintegrate and principles remain but scintillating axioms. Thus necessity enlisted executive talent and produced the politician, who, having once achieved an organization, remained at his post to keep it intact between elections and used it for purposes not always prompted by the public welfare.

In colonial days, when the struggle began between Crown and Colonist, the colonial patriots formed clubs to designate their candidates for public office. In Massachusetts these clubs were known as "caucuses," a word whose derivation is unknown, but which has now become fixed in our political vocabulary. These early caucuses in Boston have been described as follows: "Mr.

Samuel Adams' father and twenty others, one or two from the north end of the town, where all the ship business is carried on, used to meet, make a caucus, and lay their plans for introducing certain persons into places of trust and power. When they had settled it, they separated, and used each their particular influence within his own circle. He and his friends would furnish themselves with ballots, including the names of the parties fixed upon, which they distributed on the day of election. By acting in concert together with a careful and extensive distribution of ballots they generally carried the elections to their own mind."

As the revolutionary propaganda increased in momentum, caucuses assumed a more open character. They were a sort of informal town meeting, where neighbors met and agreed on candidates and the means of electing them. After the adoption of the Constitution, the same methods were continued, though modified to suit the needs of the new party alignments. In this informal manner, local and even congressional candidates were named.

Washington was the unanimous choice of the nation. In the third presidential election, John

Adams was the tacitly accepted candidate of the
Federalists and Jefferson of the Democratic-
Republicans, and no formal nominations seem to
have been made. But from 1800 to 1824 the
presidential candidates were designated by members of Congress in caucus. It was by this means
that the Virginia Dynasty fastened itself upon
the country. The congressional caucus, which was
one of the most arrogant and compact political
machines that our politics has produced, discredited itself by nominating William H. Crawford (1824), a machine politician, whom the public
never believed to be of presidential caliber. In
the bitter fight that placed John Quincy Adams
in the White House and made Jackson the eternal
enemy of Clay, the congressional caucus met its
doom. For several years, presidential candidates
were nominated by various informal methods. In
1828 a number of state legislatures formally
nominated Jackson. In several States the party
members of the legislatures in caucus nominated
presidential candidates. DeWitt Clinton was so
designated by the New York legislature in 1812
and Henry Clay by the Kentucky legislature in
1822. Great mass meetings, often garnished with
barbecues, were held in many parts of the country

in 1824 for indorsing the informal nominations of the various candidates.

But none of these methods served the purpose. The President was a national officer, backed by a national party, and chosen by a national electorate. A national system of nominating the presidential candidates was demanded. On September 26, 1831, 113 delegates of the Anti-Masonic party, representing thirteen States, met in a national convention in Baltimore. This was the first national nominating convention held in America.

In February, 1831, the Whig members of the Maryland legislature issued a call for a national Whig convention. This was held in Baltimore the following December. Eighteen States were represented by delegates, each according to the number of presidential electoral votes it cast. Clay was named for President. The first national Democratic convention met in Baltimore on May 21, 1832, and nominated Jackson.

Since that time, presidential candidates have been named in national conventions. There have been surprisingly few changes in procedure since the first convention. It opened with a temporary organization, examined the credentials of delegates, and appointed a committee on permanent organization, which reported a roster of permanent officers. It appointed a committee on platform — then called an address to the people; it listened to eulogistic nominating speeches, balloted for candidates, and selected a committee to notify the nominees of their designation. This is practically the order of procedure today. The national convention is at once the supreme court and the supreme legislature of the national party. It makes its own rules, designates its committees, formulates their procedure and defines their power, writes the platform, and appoints the national executive committee.

Two rules that have played a significant part in these conventions deserve special mention. The first Democratic convention, in order to insure the nomination of Van Buren for Vice-President — the nomination of Jackson for President was uncontested — adopted the rule that "two-thirds of the whole number of the votes in the convention shall be necessary to constitute a choice." This "two-thirds" rule, so undemocratic in its nature, remains the practice of the Democratic party today. The Whigs and Republicans always adhered to the majority rule. The early Democratic conventions also adopted the practice of allowing the

majority of the delegates from any State to cast
the vote of the entire delegation from that State,
a rule which is still adhered to by the Democrats.
But the Republicans have since 1876 adhered to
the policy of allowing each individual delegate to
cast his vote as he chooses.

The convention was by no means novel when
accepted as a national organ for a national party.
As early as 1789 an informal convention was held
in the Philadelphia State House for nominating Federalist candidates for the legislature. The
practice spread to many Pennsylvania counties
and to other States, and soon this informality of
self-appointed delegates gave way to delegates
appointed according to accepted rules. When
the legislative caucus as a means for nominating
state officers fell into disrepute, state nominating
conventions took its place. In 1812 one of the
earliest movements for a state convention was
started by Tammany Hall, because it feared that
the legislative caucus would nominate DeWitt
Clinton, its bitterest foe. The caucus, however,
did not name Clinton, and the convention was
not assembled. The first state nominating convention was held in Utica, New York, in 1824 by
that faction of the Democratic party calling itself

the People's party. The custom soon spread to
every State, so that by 1835 it was firmly established. County and city conventions also took the
place of the caucus for naming local candidates.

But nominations are only the beginning of the
contest, and obviously caucuses and conventions
cannot conduct campaigns. So from the beginning these nominating bodies appointed campaign
committees. With the increase in population
came the increased complexity of the committee system. By 1830 many of the States had
perfected a series of state, district, and county
committees.

There remained the necessity of knitting these
committees into a national unity. The national
convention which nominated Clay in 1831 appointed a "Central State Corresponding Committee"
in each State where none existed, and it recommended "to the several States to organize sub-
ordinate corresponding committees in each county
and town." This was the beginning of what soon
was to evolve into a complete national hierarchy
of committees. In 1848 the Democratic convention appointed a permanent national committee,
composed of one member from each State. This
committee was given the power to call the next

national convention, and from the start became the national executive body of the party.

It is a common notion that the politician and his machine are of comparatively recent origin. But the American politician arose contemporaneously with the party, and with such singular fecundity of ways and means that it is doubtful if his modern successors could teach him anything new. McMaster declares: "A very little study of long-forgotten politics will suffice to show that in filibustering and gerrymandering, in stealing governorships and legislatures, in using force at the polls, in colonizing and in distributing patronage to whom patronage is due, in all the frauds and tricks that go to make up the worst form of practical politics, the men who founded our state and national governments were always our equals, and often our masters." And this at a time when only propertied persons could vote in any of the States and when only professed Christians could either vote or hold office in two of them!

While Washington was President, Tammany Hall, the first municipal machine, began its career; and presently George Clinton, Governor of New York, and his nephew, DeWitt Clinton, were busy

organizing the first state machine. The Clintons
achieved their purpose through the agency of a
Council of Appointment, prescribed by the first
Constitution of the State, consisting of the Governor and four senators chosen by the legislature.
This council had the appointment of nearly all
the civil officers of the State from Secretary of
State to justices of the peace and auctioneers,
making a total of 8287 military and 6663 civil
offices. As the emoluments of some of these
offices were relatively high, the disposal of such
patronage was a plum-tree for the politician. The
Clintons had been Anti-Federalists and had
opposed the adoption of the Constitution. In
1801 DeWitt Clinton became a member of the
Council of Appointment and soon dictated its
action. The head of every Federalist office-holder
fell. Sheriffs, county clerks, surrogates, recorders,
justices by the dozen, auctioneers by the score,
were proscribed for the benefit of the Clintons.
De Witt was sent to the United States Senate in
1802, and at the age of thirty-three he found himself on the highroad to political eminence. But he
resigned almost at once to become Mayor of New
York City, a position he occupied for about ten
years, years filled with the most venomous fights

between Burrites and Bucktails. Clinton organized a compact machine in the city. A biased contemporary description of this machine has come down to us. "You [Clinton] are encircled by a mercenary band, who, while they offer adulation to your system of error, are ready at the first favorable moment to forsake and desert you. A portion of them are needy young men, who without maturely investigating the consequence, have sacrificed principle to self-aggrandizement. Others are mere parasites, that well know the tenure on which they hold their offices, and will ever pay implicit obedience to those who administer to their wants. Many of your followers are among the most profligate of the community. They are the bane of social and domestic happiness, senile and dependent panderers."

In 1812 Clinton became a candidate for President and polled 89 electoral votes against Madison's 128. Subsequently he became Governor of New York on the Erie Canal issue; but his political cunning seems to have forsaken him; and his perennial quarrels with every other faction in his State made him the object of a constant fire of vituperation. He had, however, taught all his enemies the value of spoils, and he adhered to the end to the political action he early advised a friend to adopt: "In a political warfare, the defensive side will eventually lose. The meekness of Quakerism will do in religion but not in politics. I repeat it, everything will answer to energy and decision."

Martin Van Buren was an early disciple of Clinton. Though he broke with his political chief in 1813, he had remained long enough in the Clinton school to learn every trick; and he possessed such native talent for intrigue, so smooth a manner, and such a wonderful memory for names, that he soon found himself at the head of a much more perfect and far-reaching machine than Clinton had ever dreamed of. The Empire State has never produced the equal of Van Buren as a manipulator of legislatures. No modern politician would wish to face publicity if he resorted to the petty tricks that Van Buren used in legislative politics. And when, in 1821, he was elected to the Senate of the United States, he became one of the organizers of the first national machine.

The state machine of Van Buren was long known as the "Albany Regency." It included several very able politicians: William L. Marcy, who became United States Senator in 1831; Silas Wright, elected Senator in 1833; John A. Dix, who became Senator in 1845; Benjamin F. Butler, who was United States Attorney-General under President Van Buren, besides a score or more of prominent state officials. It had an influential organ in the *Albany Argus*, lieutenants in every county, and captains in every town. Its confidential agents kept the leaders constantly informed of the political situation in every locality; and its discipline made the wish of Van Buren and his colleagues a command. Federal and local patronage and a sagacious distribution of state contracts sustained this combination. When the practice of nominating by conventions began, the Regency at once discerned the strategic value of controlling delegates, and, until the break in the Democratic party in 1848, it literally reigned in the State.

With the disintegration of the Federalist party came the loss of concentrated power by the colonial families of New England and New York. The old aristocracy of the South was more fortunate in the maintenance of its power. Jefferson's party was not only well disciplined; it gave its confidence to a people still accustomed to class rule and in turn was supported by them. In a strict sense the Virginia Dynasty was not a machine like

Van Buren's Albany Regency. It was the effect
of the concentrated influence of men of great
ability rather than a definite organization. The
congressional caucus was the instrument through
which their influence was made practical. In
1816, however, a considerable movement was
started to end the Virginia monopoly. It spread
to the Jeffersonians of the North. William H.
Crawford, of Georgia, and Daniel Tompkins, of
New York, came forward as competitors with
Monroe for the caucus nomination. The knowledge of this intrigue fostered the rising revolt
against the caucus. Twenty-two Republicans,
many of whom were known to be opposed to the
caucus system, absented themselves. Monroe
was nominated by the narrow margin of eleven
votes over Crawford. By the time Monroe had
served his second term the discrediting of the
caucus was made complete by the nomination of
Crawford by a thinly attended gathering of his
adherents, who presumed to act for the party.
The Virginia Dynasty had no further favorites to
foster, and a new political force swept into power
behind the dominating personality of Andrew
Jackson.

The new Democracy, however, did not remove

the aristocratic power of the slaveholder; and from Jackson's day to Buchanan's this became an increasing force in the party councils. The slavery question illustrates how a compact group of capable and determined men, dominated by an economic motive, can exercise for years in the political arena a preponderating influence, even though they represent an actual minority of the nation. This untoward condition was made possible by the political sagacity and persistence of the party managers and by the unwillingness of a large portion of the people to bring the real issue to a head.

Before the Civil War, then, party organization had become a fixed and necessary incident in American politics. The war changed the face of our national affairs. The changes wrought multiplied the opportunities of the professional politician, and in these opportunities, as well as in the transfused energies and ideals of the people, we must seek the causes for those perversions of party and party machinery which have characterized our modern epoch.

3

CHAPTER III

THE TIDE OF MATERIALISM

The Civil War, which shocked the country into a new national consciousness and rearranged the elements of its economic life, also brought about a new era in political activity and management. The United States after Appomattox was a very different country from the United States before Sumter was fired upon. The war was a continental upheaval, like the Appalachian uplift in our geological history, producing sharp and profound readjustments.

Despite the fact that in 1864 Lincoln had been elected on a Union ticket supported by War Democrats, the Republicans claimed the triumphs of the war as their own. They emerged from the struggle with the enormous prestige of a party triumphant and with "Saviors of the Union" inscribed on their banners.

The death of their wise and great leader opened

the door to a violent partizan orgy. President
Andrew Johnson could not check the fury of the
radical reconstructionists; and a new political era
began in a riot of dogmatic and insolent dictator-
ship, which was intensified by the mob of carpet-
baggers, scalawags, and freedmen in the South,
and not abated by the lawless promptings of the
Ku-Klux to regain patrician leadership in the
home of secession nor by the baneful resentment
of the North. The soldier was made a political
asset. For a generation the "bloody shirt" was
waved before the eyes of the Northern voter; and
the evils, both grotesque and gruesome, of an
unnatural reconstruction are not yet forgotten in
the South.

A second opportunity of the politician was
found in the rapid economic expansion that
followed the war. The feeling of security in the
North caused by the success of the Union arms
buoyed an unbounded optimism which made it
easy to enlist capital in new enterprises, and the
protective tariff and liberal banking law stimulated industry. Exports of raw material and
food products stimulated mining, grazing, and
farming.   European capital sought investments
in American railroads, mines, and industrial under-

takings.   In the decade following the war the out-
put of pig iron doubled, that of coal multiplied by
five, and that of steel by one hundred.   Superior
iron and copper, Pennsylvania coal and oil, Nevada
and California gold and silver, all yielded their
enormous values to this new call of enterprise.   In-
ventions and manufactures of all kinds flourished.
During 1850–60 manufacturing establishments had
increased by fourteen per cent.   During 1860–70
they increased seventy-nine per cent.

The Homestead Act of May 20, 1862, opened
vast areas of public lands to a new immigration.
The flow of population was westward, and the
West called for communication with the East.   The
Union Pacific and Central Pacific railways, the pioneer transcontinental lines, fostered on generous
grants of land, were the tokens of the new transportation movement.   Railroads were pushing forward everywhere with unheard-of rapidity.   Short
lines were being merged into far-reaching systems.
In the early seventies the Pennsylvania system
was organized and the Vanderbilts acquired control of lines as far west as Chicago.   Soon the
Baltimore and Ohio system extended its empire
of trade to the Mississippi.   Half a dozen ambitious trans-Mississippi systems, connecting with

four new transcontinental projects, were put into operation.

Prosperity is always the opportunity of the politician. What is of greatest significance to the student of politics is that prosperity at this time was organized on a new basis. Before the war business had been conducted largely by individuals or partnerships. The unit was small; the amount of capital needed was limited. But now the unit was expanding so rapidly, the need for capital was so lavish, the empire of trade so extensive, that a new mechanism of ownership was necessary. This device, of course, was the corporation. It had, indeed, existed as a trading unit for many years. But the corporation before 1860 was comparatively small and was generally based upon charters granted by special act of the legislature.

No other event has had so practical a bearing on our politics and our economic and social life as the advent of the corporate device for owning and manipulating private business. For it links the omnipotence of the State to the limitations of private ownership; it thrusts the interests of private business into every legislature that grants charters or passes regulating acts; it diminishes, on the other hand, that stimulus to honesty and correct dealing which a private individual discerns to be his greatest asset in trade, for it replaces individual responsibility with group responsibility and scatters ownership among so large a number of persons that sinister manipulation is possible.

But if the private corporation, through its interest in broad charter privileges and liberal corporation laws and its devotion to the tariff and to conservative financial policies, found it convenient to do business with the politician and his organization, the quasi-public corporations, especially the steam railroads and street railways, found it almost essential to their existence. They received not only their franchises but frequently large bonuses from the public treasury. The Pacific roads alone were endowed with an empire of 145,000,000 acres of public land. States, counties, and cities freely loaned their credit and gave ample charters to new railway lines which were to stimulate prosperity.

City councils, legislatures, mayors, governors, Congress, and presidents were drawn into the maelstrom of commercialism. It is not surprising that side by side with the new business organization there grew up a new political organization, and that the new business magnate was accompanied by a new political magnate. The party machine and the party boss were the natural product of the time, which was a time of gain and greed. It was a sordid reaction, indeed, from the high principles that sought victory on the field of battle and that found their noblest embodiment in the character of Abraham Lincoln.

The dominant and domineering party chose the leading soldier of the North as its candidate for President. General Grant, elected as a popular idol because of his military genius, possessed neither the experience nor the skill to countermove the machinations of designing politicians and their business allies. On the other hand, he soon displayed an admiration for business success that placed him at once in accord with the spirit of the hour. He exalted men who could make money rather than men who could command ideas. He chose Alexander T. Stewart, the New York merchant prince, one of the three richest men of his day, for Secretary of the Treasury. The law, however, forbade the appointment to this office of any one who should "directly or indirectly be concerned or interested in carrying on the business of trade or commerce," and Stewart was disqualified. Adolph E. Borie of Philadelphia, whose

qualifications were the possession of great wealth
and the friendship of the President, was named
Secretary of the Navy. Another personal friend,
John A. Rawlins, was named Secretary of War.
A third friend, Elihu B. Washburne of Illinois,
was made Secretary of State. Washburne soon
resigned, and Hamilton Fish of New York was appointed in his place. Fish, together with General
Jacob D. Cox of Ohio, Secretary of the Interior,
and Judge E. Rockwood Hoar of Massachusetts,
Attorney-General, formed a strong triumvirate of
ability and character in the Cabinet. But, while
Grant displayed pleasure in the companionship
of these eminent men, they never possessed his
complete confidence. When the machinations for
place and favor began, Hoar and Cox were in
the way. Hoar had offended the Senate in his
recommendations for federal circuit judges (the
circuit court was then newly established), and
when the President named him for Justice of
the Supreme Court, Hoar was rejected. Senator
Cameron, one of the chief spoils politicians of
the time, told Hoar frankly why: "What could
you expect for a man who had snubbed seventy
Senators!"   A few months later (June, 1870), the
President bluntly asked for Hoar's resignation,

a sacrifice to the gods of the Senate, to purchase their favor for the Santo Domingo treaty.

Cox resigned in the autumn. As Secretary of the Interior he had charge of the Patent Office, Census Bureau, and Indian Service, all of them requiring many appointments. He had attempted to introduce a sort of civil service examination for applicants and had vehemently protested against political assessments levied on clerks in his department. He especially offended Senators Cameron and Chandler, party chieftains who had the ear of the President. General Cox stated the matter plainly: "My views of the necessity of reform in the civil service had brought me more or less into collision with the plans of our active political managers and my sense of duty has obliged me to oppose some of their methods of action."

These instances reveal how the party chieftains insisted inexorably upon their demands. To them the public service was principally a means to satisfy party ends, and the chief duty of the President and his Cabinet was to satisfy the claims of party necessity. General Cox said that distributing offices occupied "the larger part of the time of the President and all his Cabinet." General Garfield wrote (1877): "One-third of the working hours of Senators and Representatives is hardly sufficient to meet the demands made upon them in reference to appointments to office."

By the side of the partizan motives stalked the desire for gain. There were those to whom parties meant but the opportunity for sudden wealth. The President's admiration for commercial success and his inability to read the motives of sycophants multiplied their opportunities, and in the eight years of his administration there was consummated the baneful union of business and politics.

During the second Grant campaign (1872), when Horace Greeley was making his astounding run for President, the New York *Sun* hinted at gross and wholesale briberies of Congressmen by Oakes Ames and his associates who had built the Union Pacific Railroad, an enterprise which the United States had generously aided with loans and gifts.

Three committees of Congress, two in the House and one in the Senate (the Poland Committee, the Wilson Committee, and the Senate Committee), subsequently investigated the charges. Their investigations disclosed the fact that Ames, then a member of the House of Representatives, the

principal stockholder in the Union Pacific, and
the soul of the enterprise, had organized, under
an existing Pennsylvania charter, a construction company called the Crédit Mobilier, whose
shares were issued to Ames and his associates. To
the Crédit Mobilier were issued the bonds and
stock of the Union Pacific, which had been paid
for "at not more than thirty cents on the dollar in
road-making."[1] As the United States, in addition
to princely gifts of land, had in effect guaranteed
the cost of construction by authorizing the issue
of Government bonds, dollar for dollar and side
by side with the bonds of the road, the motive
of the magnificent shuffle, which gave the road
into the hands of a construction company, was
clear. Now it was alleged that stock of the Crédit
Mobilier, paying dividends of three hundred and
forty per cent, had been distributed by Ames
among many of his fellow-Congressmen, in order
to forestall a threatened investigation.   It was disclosed that some of the members had refused point
blank to have anything to do with the stock; others
had refused after deliberation; others had purchased
some of it outright; others, alas! had "purchased"
it, to be paid for out of its own dividends.

[1] Testimony before the Wilson Committee.

The majority of the members involved in the nasty affair were absolved by the Poland Committee from "any corrupt motive or purpose." But Oakes Ames of Massachusetts and James Brooks of New York were recommended for expulsion from the House and Patterson of New Hampshire from the Senate. The House, however, was content with censuring Ames and Brooks, and the Senate permitted Patterson's term to expire, since only five days of it remained. Whatever may have been the opinion of Congress, and whatever a careful reading of the testimony discloses to an impartial mind at this remote day, upon the voters of that time the revelations came as a shock. Some of the most trusted Congressmen were drawn into the miasma of suspicion, among them Garfield; Dawes; Scofield; Wilson, the newly elected Vice-President; Colfax, the outgoing Vice-President. Colfax had been a popular idol, with the Presidency in his vision; now bowed and disgraced, he left the national capital never to return with a public commission.

In 1874 came the disclosures of the Whiskey Ring. They involved United States Internal Revenue officers and distillers in the revenue district of St. Louis and a number of officials at Washington. Benjamin H. Bristow, on becoming Secretary of the Treasury in June of that year, immediately scented corruption. He discovered that during 1871–74 only about one-third of the whiskey shipped from St. Louis had paid the tax and that the Government had been defrauded of nearly $3,000,000. "If a distiller was honest," says James Ford Rhodes, the eminent historian, "he was entrapped into some technical violation of the law by the officials, who by virtue of their authority seized his distillery, giving him the choice of bankruptcy or a partnership in their operations; and generally he succumbed."

McDonald, the supervisor of the St. Louis revenue district, was the leader of the Whiskey Ring. He lavished gifts upon President Grant, who, with an amazing indifference and innocence, accepted such favors from all kinds of sources. Orville E. Babcock, the President's private secretary, who possessed the complete confidence of the guileless general, was soon enmeshed in the net of investigation. Grant at first declared, "If Babcock is guilty, there is no man who wants him so much proven guilty as I do, for it is the greatest piece of traitorism to me that a man could possibly practice." When Babcock was indicted, however, for complicity to defraud the Government, the President did not hesitate to say on oath that he had never seen anything in Babcock's behavior which indicated that he was in any way interested in the Whiskey Ring and that he had always had "great confidence in his integrity and efficiency." In other ways the President displayed his eagerness to defend his private secretary. The jury acquitted Babcock, but the public did not. He was compelled to resign under pressure of public condemnation, and was afterwards indicted for conspiracy to rob a safe of documents of an incriminating character. But Grant seems never to have lost faith in him. Three of the men sent to prison for their complicity in the whiskey fraud were pardoned after six months. McDonald, the chieftain of the gang, served but one year of his term.

The exposure of the Whiskey Ring was followed by an even more startling humiliation. The House Committee on Expenditures in the War Department recommended that General William W. Belknap, Secretary of War, be impeached for "high crimes and misdemeanors while in office," and the House unanimously adopted the recommendation. The evidence upon which the committee based its drastic recommendation disclosed the most sordid division of spoils between the Secretary and his wife and two rascals who held in succession the valuable post of trader at Fort Sill in the Indian Territory.

The committee's report was read about three o'clock in the afternoon of March 2, 1876. In the forenoon of the same day Belknap had sent his resignation to the President, who had accepted it immediately. The President and Belknap were personal friends. But the certainty of Belknap's perfidy was not removed by the attitude of the President, nor by the vote of the Senate on the article of impeachment — 37 guilty, 25 not guilty — for the evidence was too convincing. The public knew by this time Grant's childlike failing in sticking to his friends; and 23 of the 25 Senators who voted not guilty had publicly declared they did so, not because they believed him innocent, but because they believed they had no jurisdiction over an official who had resigned.

There were many minor indications of the harvest which gross materialism was reaping in the political field. State and city governments were surrendered to political brigands. In 1871 the Governor of Nebraska was removed for embezzlement. Kansas was startled by revelations of brazen bribery in her senatorial elections (1872–1873). General Schenck, representing the United States at the Court of St. James, humiliated his country by dabbling in a fraudulent mining scheme.

In a speech before the Senate, then trying General Belknap, Senator George F. Hoar, on May 6, 1876, summed up the greater abominations:

My own public life has been a very brief and insignificant one, extending little beyond the duration of a single term of senatorial office. But in that brief period I have seen five judges of a high court of the United States driven from office by threats of impeachment for corruption or maladministration. I have heard the taunt from friendliest lips, that when the United States presented herself in the East to take part with the civilized world in generous competition in the arts of life, the only products of her institutions in which she surpassed all others beyond question was her corruption. I have seen in the State in the Union foremost in power and wealth four judges of her courts impeached for corruption, and the political administration of her chief city become a disgrace and a byword throughout the world. I have seen the chairman of

the Committee on Military Affairs in the House rise
in his place and demand the expulsion of four of his
associates for making sale of their official privilege of
selecting the youths to be educated at our great military
schools.   When the greatest railroad of the world,
binding together the continent and uniting the two
great seas which wash our shores, was finished, I have
seen our national triumph and exaltation turned to
bitterness and shame by the unanimous reports of three
committees of Congress — two in the House and one
here — that every step of that mighty enterprise had
been taken in fraud.   I have heard in highest places the
shameless doctrine avowed by men grown old in public
office that the true way by which power should be
gained in the Republic is to bribe the people with the
offices created for their service, and the true end for
which it should be used when gained is the promotion
of selfish ambition and the gratification of personal
revenge.   I have heard that suspicions haunt the foot-
steps of the trusted companions of the President.

These startling facts did not shatter the prestige
of the Republicans, the "Saviors of the Union,"
nor humble their leaders.   One of them, Senator
Foraker, says[1]: "The campaign (1876) on the part
of the Democrats gave emphasis to the reform idea
and exploited Tilden as the great reform governor of New York and the best fitted man in the
country to bring about reforms in the Government

[1] *Notes from a Busy Life*, vol. i., 98.

4

of the United States.   No reforms were needed:
but a fact like that never interfered with a reform campaign." The orthodoxy of the politician
remained unshaken.   Foraker's reasons were the
creed of thousands: "The Republican party had
prosecuted the war successfully; had reconstructed
the States; had rehabilitated our finances, and
brought on specie redemption." The memoirs
of politicians and statesmen of this period, such
as Cullom, Foraker, Platt, even Hoar, are imbued
with an inflexible faith in the party and colored
by the conviction that it is a function of Government to aid business. Platt, for instance, alluding
to Blaine's attitude as Speaker, in the seventies,
said: "What I liked about him was his frank and
persistent contention that the citizen who best
loved his party and was loyal to it, was loyal to
and best loved his country." And many years
afterwards, when a new type of leader appeared
representing a new era of conviction, Platt was
deeply concerned. His famous letter to Roosevelt, when the Rough Rider was being mentioned
for Governor of New York (1899), shows the
reluctance of the old man to see the signs of the
times: "The thing that really did bother me was
this: I had heard from a great many sources that

you were a little loose on the relations of capital and labor, on trusts and combinations, and indeed on the numerous questions which have recently arisen in politics affecting the security of earnings and the right of a man to run his own business in his own way, with due respect of course to the Ten Commandments and the Penal Code."

The leaders of both the great parties firmly and honestly believed that it was the duty of the Government to aid private enterprise, and that by stimulating business everybody is helped. This article of faith, with the doctrine of the sanctity of the party, was a natural product of the conditions outlined in the beginning of this chapter — the war and the remarkable economic expansion following the war. It was the cause of the alliance between business and politics. It made the machine and the boss the sinister and ever present shadows of legitimate organization and leadership.

CHAPTER IV

THE POLITICIAN AND THE CITY

THE gigantic national machine that was erected during Grant's administration would have been ineffectual without local sources of power. These sources of power were found in the cities, now thriving on the new-born commerce and industry, increasing marvelously in numbers and in size, and offering to the political manipulator opportunities that have rarely been paralleled.[1]

The governmental framework of the American city is based on the English system as exemplified

[1] Between 1860 and 1890 the number of cities of 8000 or more inhabitants increased from 141 to 448, standing at 226 in 1870. In 1865 less than 20% of our people lived in the cities; in 1890, over 30%; in 1900, 40%; in 1910, 46.3%. By 1890 there were six cities with more than half a million inhabitants; fifteen with more than 200,000, and twenty-eight with more than 100,000. In 1910 there were twenty-eight cities with a population over 200,000, fifty cities over 100,000, and ninety-eight over 50,000. It was no uncommon occurrence for a city to double its population in a decade. In ten years Birmingham gained 245%, Los Angeles, 211%, Seattle, 194%, Spokane, 183%, Dallas, 116%, Schenectady, 129%.

in the towns of Colonial America. Their charters were received from the Crown and their business was conducted by a mayor and a council composed of aldermen and councilmen. The mayor was usually appointed; the council elected by a property-holding electorate. In New England the glorified town meeting was an important agency of local government.

After the Revolution, mayors as well as councilmen were elected, and the charters of the towns were granted by the legislature, not by the executive, of the State. In colonial days charters had been granted by the King. They had fixed for the city certain immunities and well-defined spheres of autonomy. But when the legislatures were given the power to grant charters, they reduced the charter to the level of a statutory enactment, which could be amended or repealed by any successive legislature, thereby opening up a convenient field for political maneuvering. The courts have, moreover, construed these charters strictly, holding the cities closely bound to those powers which the legislatures conferred upon them.

The task of governing the early American town was simple enough. In 1790 New York, Phila-

delphia, Boston, Baltimore, and Charleston were
the only towns in the United States of over 8000
inhabitants; all together they numbered scarcely
130,000. Their populations were homogeneous;
their wants were few; and they were still in that
happy childhood when every voter knew nearly
every other voter and when everybody knew his
neighbor's business as well as his own, and perhaps better.

Gradually the towns awoke to their newer
needs and demanded public service — lighting,
street cleaning, fire protection, public education.
All these matters, however, could be easily looked
after by the mayor and the council committees.
But when these towns began to spread rapidly
into cities, they quickly outgrew their colonial
garments. Yet the legislatures were loath to cast
the old garments aside. One may say that from
1840 to 1901, when the Galveston plan of commission government was inaugurated, American
municipal government was nothing but a series
of contests between a small body of alert citizens attempting to fix responsibility on public
officers and a few adroit politicians attempting
to elude responsibility; both sides appealing to an
electorate which was habitually somnolent but

subject to intermittent awakenings through spasms of righteousness.

During this epoch no important city remained immune from ruthless legislative interference. Year after year the legislature shifted officers and responsibilities at the behest of the boss. "Ripper bills" were passed, tearing up the entire administrative systems of important municipalities. The city was made the plaything of the boss and the machine.

Throughout the constant shifts that our city governments have undergone one may, however, discern three general plans of government.

The first was the centering of power in the city council, whether composed of two chambers — a board of aldermen and a common council — as in New York, Philadelphia, and Chicago, or of one council, as in many lesser cities. It soon became apparent that a large body, whose chief function is legislation, is utterly unfit to look after administrative details. Such a body, in order to do business, must act through committees. Responsibility is scattered. Favoritism is possible in letting contracts, in making appointments, in depositing city funds, in making public improvements, in purchasing supplies and real estate, and in a thousand other ways. So, by controlling the appointment of committees, a shrewd manipulator could virtually control all the municipal activities and make himself overlord of the city.

The second plan of government attempted to make the mayor the controlling force. It reduced the council to a legislative body and exalted the mayor into a real executive with power to appoint and to remove heads of departments, thereby making him responsible for the city administration. Brooklyn under Mayor Seth Low was an encouraging example of this type of government. But the type was rarely found in a pure form. The politician succeeded either in electing a subservient mayor or in curtailing the mayor's authority by having the heads of departments elected or appointed by the council or made subject to the approval of the council. If the council held the key to the city treasury, the boss reigned, for councilmen from properly gerrymandered wards could usually be trusted to execute his will.

The third form of government was government by boards. Here it was attempted to place the administration of various municipal activities in the hands of independent boards. Thus a board had charge of the police, another of the fire de-

partment, another of public works, and so on.
Often there were a dozen of these boards and
not infrequently over thirty in a single city, as
in Philadelphia.   Sometimes these boards were
elected by the people; sometimes they were appointed by the council; sometimes they were
appointed by the mayor; in one or two instances
they were appointed by the Governor.   Often
their powers were shared with committees of the
council; a committee on police, for instance, shared
with the Board of Police Commissioners the direction of police affairs.   Usually these boards were
responsible to no one but the electorate (and that
remotely) and were entirely without coördination,
a mere agglomeration of independent creations
generally with ill-defined powers.

Sometimes the laws provided that not all the
members of the appointive boards should "belong
to the same political party" or "be of the same
political opinion in state and national issues."   It
was clearly the intention to wipe out the partizan complexion of such boards.   But this device
was no stumbling-block to the boss.   Whatever
might be the "opinions" on national matters of
the men appointed, they usually had a perfect
understanding with the appointing authorities as

to local matters. As late as 1898, a Democratic mayor of New York (Van Wyck) summarily removed the two Republican members of the Board of Police Commissioners and replaced them by Republicans after his own heart. In truth, the bipartizan board fitted snugly into the dual party régime that existed in many cities, whereby the county offices were apportioned to one party, the city offices to the other, and the spoils to both. It is doubtful if any device was ever more deceiving and less satisfactory than the bipartizan board.

The reader must not be led to think that any one of these plans of municipal government prevailed at any one time. They all still exist, contemporaneously with the newer commission plan and the city manager plan.

Hand in hand with these experiments in governmental mechanisms for the growing cities went a rapidly increasing expenditure of public funds. Streets had to be laid out, paved, and lighted; sewers extended; fire-fighting facilities increased; schools built; parks, boulevards, and playgrounds acquired, and scores of new activities undertaken by the municipality. All these brought grist to the politician's mill. So did his control of the police force and the police courts. And finally, with the city reaching its eager streets far out into the country, came the necessity for rapid transportation, which opened up for the municipal politician a new El Dorado.

Under our laws the right of a public service corporation to occupy the public streets is based upon a franchise from the city. Before the days of the referendum the franchise was granted by the city council, usually as a monopoly, sometimes in perpetuity; and, until comparatively recent years, the corporation paid nothing to the city for the rights it acquired.

When we reflect that within a few decades of the discovery of electric power, every city, large and small, had its street-car and electric-light service, and that most of these cities, through their councils, gave away these monopoly rights for long periods of time, we can imagine the princely aggregate of the gifts which public service corporations have received at the hands of our municipal governments, and the nature of the temptations these corporations were able to spread before the greedy gaze of those whose gesture would seal the grant.

But it was not only at the granting of the

franchise that the boss and his machine sought
for spoils. A public service corporation, being
constantly asked for favors, is a continuing opportunity for the political manipulator. Public
service corporations could share their patronage with the politician in exchange for favors.
Through their control of many jobs, and through
their influence with banks, they could show a
wide assortment of favors to the politician in
return for his influence; for instance, in the matter
of traffic regulations, permission to tear up the
streets, inspection laws, rate schedules, tax assessments, coroners' reports, or juries.

When the politician went to the voters, he
adroitly concealed his designs under the name of
one of the national parties. Voters were asked
to vote for a Republican or a Democrat, not for a
policy of municipal administration or other local
policies. The system of committees, caucuses,
conventions, built up in every city, was linked
to the national organization. A citizen of New
York, for instance, was not asked to vote for the
Broadway Franchise, which raised such a scandal
in the eighties, but to vote for aldermen running
on a national tariff ticket!

The electorate was somnolent and permitted

the politician to have his way. The multitudes
of the city came principally from two sources,
from Europe and from the rural districts of our
own country. Those who came to the city from
the country were prompted by industrial motives;
they sought wider opportunities; they soon became immersed in their tasks and paid little
attention to public questions. The foreign immigrants who congested our cities were alien to
American institutions. They formed a heterogeneous population to whom a common ideal of
government was unknown and democracy a word
without meaning. These foreigners were easily
influenced and easily led. Under the old naturalization laws, they were herded into the courts
just before election and admitted to citizenship.
In New York they were naturalized under the
guidance of ward-heelers, not infrequently at
the rate of one a minute! And, before the days
of registration laws, ballots were distributed to
them and they were led to the polls, as charity
children are given excursion tickets and are led
to their annual summer's day picnic.

The slipshod methods of naturalization have
been revealed since the new law (1906) has been
in force. Tens of thousands of voters who thought

they were citizens found that their papers were only declarations of intentions, or "first papers." Other tens of thousands had lost even these papers and could not designate the courts that had issued them; and other thousands found that the courts that had naturalized them were without jurisdiction in the matter.

It was not merely among these newcomers that the boss found his opportunities for carrying elections. The dense city blocks were convenient lodging places for "floaters." Just before elections, the population of the downtown wards in the larger cities increased surprisingly. The boss fully availed himself of the psychological and social reactions of the city upon the individual, knowing instinctively how much more easily men are corrupted when they are merged in the crowd and have lost their sense of personal responsibility.

It was in the city, then, that industrial politics found their natural habitat. We shall now scrutinize more closely some of the developments which arose out of such an environment.

CHAPTER V

TAMMANY HALL

BEFORE the Revolutionary War numerous societies were organized to aid the cause of Independence. These were sometimes called "Sons of Liberty" and not infrequently "Sons of St. Tammany," after an Indian brave whom tradition had shrouded in virtue. The name was probably adopted to burlesque the royalist societies named after St. George, St. David, or St. Andrew. After the war these societies vanished. But, in New York City, William Mooney, an upholsterer, reorganized the local society as "Tammany Society or Columbian Order," devoted ostensibly to good-fellowship and charity. Its officers bore Indian titles and its ceremonies were more or less borrowed from the red man, not merely because of their unique and picturesque character, but to emphasize the truly American and anti-British convictions of its members.

The society attracted that element of the town's population which delighted in the crude ceremonials and the stimulating potions that always accompanied them, mostly small shopkeepers and mechanics.   It was among this class that the spirit of discontent against the power of Federalism was strongest — a spirit that has often become decisive in our political fortunes.

This was still the day of the "gentleman," of small clothes, silver shoe-buckles, powdered wigs, and lace ruffles.   Only taxpayers and propertied persons could vote, and public office was still invested with certain prerogatives and privileges. Democracy was little more than a name.   There was, however, a distinct division of sentiment, and the drift towards democracy was accelerated by immigration.   The newcomers were largely of the humble classes, among whom the doctrines of democratic discontent were welcome.

Tammany soon became partizan.   The Federalist members withdrew, probably influenced by Washington's warning against secret political societies.   By 1798 it was a Republican club meeting in various taverns, finally selecting Martling's "Long Room" for its nightly carousals. Soon after this a new constitution was adopted which adroitly transformed the society into a compact political machine, every member subscribing to the oath that he would resist the encroachments of centralized power over the State.

Tradition has it that the transformer of Tammany into the first compact and effective political machine was Aaron Burr. There is no direct evidence that he wrote the new constitution. But there is collateral evidence. Indeed, it would not have been Burrian had he left any written evidence of his connection with the organization. For Burr was one of those intriguers who revel in mystery, who always hide their designs, and never bind themselves in writing without leaving a dozen loopholes for escape. He was by this time a prominent figure in American politics. His skill had been displayed in Albany, both in the passing of legislation and in out-maneuvering Hamilton and having himself elected United States Senator against the powerful combination of the Livingstons and the Schuylers. He was plotting for the Presidency as the campaign of 1800 approached, and Tammany was to be the fulcrum to lift him to this conspicuous place.

Under the ostensible leadership of Matthew L.

Davis, Burr's chief lieutenant, every ward of the city was carefully organized, a polling list was made, scores of new members were pledged to Tammany, and during the three days of voting (in New York State until 1840 elections lasted three days), while Hamilton was making eloquent speeches for the Federalists, Burr was secretly manipulating the wires of his machine. Burr and Tammany won in New York City, though Burr failed to win the Presidency. The political career of this remarkable organization, which has survived over one hundred and twenty years of stormy history, was now well launched.

From that time to the present the history of Tammany Hall is a tale of victories, followed by occasional disclosures of corruption and favoritism; of quarrels with governors and presidents; of party fights between "up-state" and "city"; of skulking when its sachems were unwelcome in the White House; of periodical displays of patriotism for cloaking its grosser crimes; of perennial charities for fastening itself more firmly on the poorer populace which has always been the source of its power; of colossal municipal enterprise for profit-sharing; and of a continuous political efficiency due to sagacious leadership, a remarkable adaptability to the necessities of the hour, and a patience that outlasts every "reform."

It early displayed all the traits that have made it successful. In 1801, for the purpose of carrying city elections, it provided thirty-nine men with money to purchase houses and lots in one ward, and seventy men with money for the same purpose in another ward, thus manufacturing freeholders for polling purposes. In 1806 Benjamin Romaine, a grand sachem, was removed from the office of city controller by his own party for acquiring land from the city without paying for it. In 1807 several superintendents of city institutions were dismissed for frauds. The inspector of bread, a sachem, resigned because his threat to extort one-third of the fees from his subordinates had become public. Several assessment collectors, all prominent in Tammany, were compelled to reimburse the city for deficits in their accounts. One of the leading aldermen used his influence to induce the city to sell land to his brother-in-law at a low price, and then bade the city buy it back for many times its value. Mooney, the founder of the society, now superintendent of the almshouse, was caught in a characteristic fraud. His salary was $1000 a year, with

$500 for family expenses. But it was discovered that his "expenses" amounted to $4000 a year, and that he had credited to himself on the books $1000 worth of supplies and numerous sums for "trifles for Mrs. Mooney."

In September, 1826, the Grand Jury entered an indictment against Matthew L. Davis and a number of other Tammany men for defrauding several banks and insurance companies of over $2,000,000. This created a tremendous sensation. Political influence was at once set in motion, and only the minor defendants were sent to the penitentiary.

In 1829 Samuel Swartwout, one of the Tammany leaders, was appointed Collector of the Port of New York. His downfall came in 1838, and he fled to Europe. His defalcations in the Custom House were found to be over $1,222,700; and "to Swartwout" became a useful phrase until Tweed's day. He was succeeded by Jesse Hoyt, another sachem and notorious politician, against whom several judgments for default were recorded in the Superior Court, which were satisfied very soon after his appointment. At this time another Tammany chieftain, W. M. Price, United States District Attorney for Southern New York, defaulted for $75,000.

It was in 1851 that the council commonly known as "The Forty Thieves" was elected. In it William M. Tweed served his apprenticeship. Some of the maneuvers of this council and of other officials were divulged by a Grand Jury in its presentment of February 23, 1853. The presentment states: "It was clearly shown that enormous sums of money were spent for the procurement of railroad grants in the city, and that towards the decision and procurement of the Eighth Avenue railway grant, a sum so large that would startle the most credulous was expended; but in consequence of the voluntary absence of important witnesses, the Grand Jury was left without direct testimony of the particular recipients of the different amounts."

These and other exposures brought on a number of amendments to the city charter, surrounding with greater safeguards the sale or lease of city property and the letting of contracts; and a reform council was elected. Immediately upon the heels of this reform movement followed the shameful régime of Fernando Wood, an able, crafty, unscrupulous politician, who began by announcing himself a reformer, but who soon became a boss in the most offensive sense of that term — not, however, in Tammany Hall, for he was ousted from that organization after his reëlection as mayor in 1856. He immediately organized a machine of his own, Mozart Hall. The intense struggle between the two machines cost the city a great sum, for the taxpayers were mulcted to pay the bills.

Through the anxious days of the Civil War, when the minds of thoughtful citizens were occupied with national issues, the tide of reform ebbed and flowed. A reform candidate was elected mayor in 1863, but Tammany returned to power two years later by securing the election and then the reëlection of John T. Hoffman. Hoffman possessed considerable ability and an attractive personality. His zeal for high office, however, made him easily amenable to the manipulators. Tammany made him Governor and planned to name him for President. Behind his popularity, which was considerable, and screened by the greater excitements of the war, reconstruction, and the impeachment of Andrew Johnson, lurked the Ring, whose exposures and confessions were soon to amaze everyone.

The chief ringster was William M. Tweed, and his name will always be associated in the public mind with political bossdom. This is his immortality. He was a chairmaker by trade, a vulgar good fellow by nature, a politician by circumstances, a boss by evolution, and a grafter by choice. He became grand sachem of Tammany and chairman of the general committee. This committee he ruled with blunt directness. When he wanted a question carried, he failed to ask for the negative votes; and soon he was called "the Boss," a title he never resented, and which usage has since fixed in our politics. So he ruled Tammany with a high hand; made nominations arbitrarily; bullied, bought, and traded; became President of the Board of Supervisors, thus holding the key to the city's financial policies; and was elected State Senator, thereby directing the granting of legislative favors to his city and to his corporations.

In 1868 Tammany carried Hoffman into the Governor's chair, and in the following year the Democrats carried the State legislature. Tweed now had a new charter passed which virtually put New York City into his pocket by placing the finances of the metropolis entirely in the hands of a Board of Apportionment which he dominated. Of this Board, the mayor of the city was the chairman, with the power to appoint the other members. He promptly named Tweed, Connolly, and P. B. Sweeny. This was the famous Ring. The mayor was A. Oakey Hall, dubbed "Elegant Oakey" by his pals because of his fondness for clubs, society, puns, and poems; but Nast called him "O. K. Haul." Sweeny, commonly known as "Pete," was a lawyer of ability, and was generally believed to be the plotter of the quartet. Nast transformed his middle initial B. into "Brains." Connolly was just a coarse gangster.

There was some reason for the Ring's faith in its invulnerability. It controlled Governor and legislature, was formidable in the national councils of the Democratic party, and its Governor was widely mentioned for the presidential nomination. It possessed complete power over the city council, the mayor, and many of the judges. It was in partnership with Gould and Fiske of the Erie, then reaping great harvests in Wall Street, and with street railway and other public service corporations. Through untold largess it silenced rivalry from within and criticism from without. And, when suspicion first raised its voice, it adroitly invited a committee of prominent and wealthy citizens, headed by John Jacob Astor, to examine the controller's accounts. After six hours spent in the City Hall these respectable gentlemen signed an acquitment, saying that "the affairs of the city under the charge of the controller are administered in a correct and faithful manner."

Thus intrenched, the Ring levied tribute on every municipal activity. Everyone who had a charge against the city, either for work done or materials furnished, was told to add to the amount of his bill, at first 10%, later 66%, and finally 85%. One man testified that he was told to raise to $55,000 his claim of $5000. He got his $5000; the Ring got $50,000. The building of the Court House, still known as "Tweed's Court House," was estimated to cost $3,000,000, but it cost many times that sum. The item "repairing fixtures" amounted to $1,149,874.50, before the building was completed. Forty chairs and three tables cost $179,729.60; thermometers cost $7500. G. S. Miller, a carpenter, received $360,747.61, and a plasterer named Gray, $2,870,464.06 for nine months' "work." The *Times* dubbed him the "Prince of Plasterers." "A plasterer who can earn $138,187 in two days [December 20 and 21] and that in the depths of winter, need not be poor." Carpets cost $350,000, most of the Brussels and

Axminster going to the New Metropolitan Hotel just opened by Tweed's son.

The Ring's hold upon the legislature was through bribery, not through partizan adhesion. Tweed himself confessed that he gave one man in Albany $600,000 for buying votes to pass his charter; and Samuel J. Tilden estimated the total cost for this purpose at over one million dollars. Tweed said he bought five Republican senators for $40,000 apiece. The vote on the charter was 30 to 2 in the Senate, 116 to 5 in the Assembly. Similar sums were spent in Albany in securing corporate favors. The Viaduct Railway Bill is an example. This bill empowered a company, practically owned by the Ring, to build a railway on or above any street in the city. It provided that the city should subscribe for $5,000,000 of the stock; and it exempted the company from taxation. Collateral bills were introduced enabling the company to widen and grade any streets, the favorite "job" of a Tammany grafter. Fortunately for the city, exposure came before this monstrous scheme could be put in motion.

Newspapers in the city were heavily subsidized. Newspapers in Albany were paid munificently for printing. One of the Albany papers received

$207,900 for one year's work which was worth less
than $10,000. Half a dozen reporters of the lead-
ing dailies were put on the city payroll at from
$2000 to $2500 a year for "services."

The Himalayan size of these swindles and their
monumental effrontery led the New York *Sun*
humorously to suggest the erection of a statue to
the principal Robber Baron, "in commemoration
of his services to the commonwealth." A letter
was sent out asking for funds. There were a
great many men in New York, the *Sun* thought,
who would not be unwilling to refuse a contribution. But Tweed declined the honor. In its issue
of March 14, 1871, the *Sun* has this headline:

A GREAT MAN'S MODESTY

THE HON. WILLIAM M. TWEED DECLINES THE
SUN'S STATUE. CHARACTERISTIC LETTER FROM
THE GREAT NEW YORK PHILANTHROPIST. HE
THINKS THAT VIRTUE SHOULD BE ITS OWN
REWARD. THE MOST REMARKABLE LETTER EVER
WRITTEN BY THE NOBLE BENEFACTOR OF THE
PEOPLE.

Another kind of memorial to his genius for absorb-
ing the people's money was awaiting this phil-
anthropic buccaneer.

Vulgar ostentation was the outward badge of these civic burglaries. Tweed moved into a Fifth Avenue mansion and gave his daughter a wedding at which she received $100,000 worth of gifts; her wedding dress was a $5000 creation. At Greenwich he built a country estate where the stables were framed of choice mahogany. Sweeny hobnobbed with Jim Fiske of the Erie, the Tweed of Wall Street, who went about town dressed in loud checks and lived with his harem in his Opera House on Eighth Avenue.

Thoughtful citizens saw these things going on and believed the city was being robbed, but they could not prove it. There were two attacking parties, however, who did not wait for proofs — Thomas Nast, the brilliant cartoonist of *Harper's Weekly*, and the New York *Times*. The incisive cartoons of Nast appealed to the imaginations of all classes; even Tweed complained that his illiterate following could "look at the damn pictures." The trenchant editorials of Louis L. Jennings in the *Times* reached a thoughtful circle of readers. In one of these editorials, February 24, 1871, before the exposure, he said: "There is absolutely nothing — nothing in the city — which is beyond the reach of the insatiable gang who have obtained possession of it. They can get a grand jury dismissed at any time, and, as we have seen, the legislature is completely at their disposal."

Finally proof did come and, as is usual in such cases, it came from the inside. James O'Brien, an ex-sheriff and the leader in a Democratic "reform movement" calling itself "Young Democracy," secured the appointment of one of his friends as clerk in the controller's office. Transcripts of the accounts were made, and these O'Brien brought to the *Times*, which began their publication, July 8, 1871. The Ring was in consternation. It offered George Jones, the proprietor of the *Times*, $5,000,000 for his silence and sent a well-known banker to Nast with an invitation to go to Europe "to study art," with $100,000 for "expenses."

"Do you think I could get $200,000?" innocently asked Nast.

"I believe from what I have heard in the bank that you might get it."

After some reflection, the cartoonist asked: "Don't you think I could get $500,000 to make that trip?"

"You can; you can get $500,000 in gold to drop this Ring business and get out of the country."

"Well, I don't think I'll do it," laughed the artist. "I made up my mind not long ago to put some of those fellows behind the bars, and I am going to put them there."

"Only be careful, Mr. Nast, that you do not first put yourself in a coffin," said the banker as he left.

A public meeting in Cooper Institute, April 6, 1871, was addressed by William E. Dodge, Henry Ward Beecher, William M. Evarts, and William F. Havemeyer. They vehemently denounced Tweed and his gang. Tweed smiled and asked, "Well, what are you going to do about it?" On the 4th of September, the same year, a second mass meeting held in the same place answered the question by appointing a committee of seventy. Tweed, Sweeny, and Hall, now alarmed by the disclosures in the *Times*, decided to make Connolly the scapegoat, and asked the aldermen and supervisors to appoint a committee to examine his accounts. By the time the committee appeared for the examination — its purpose had been well announced — the vouchers for 1869 and 1870 had disappeared. Mayor Hall then asked for Connolly's resignation. But instead, Connolly consulted Samuel J. Tilden, who advised him to appoint Andrew H. Green, a well-known and respected citizen, as his deputy. This turned the tables on the three other members of the Ring, whose efforts to oust both Connolly and Green were unavailing. In this manner the citizens got control of the treasury books, and the Grand Jury began its inquisitions. Sweeny and Connolly soon fled to Europe. Sweeny afterwards settled for $400,000 and returned. Hall's case was presented to a grand jury which proved to be packed. A new panel was ordered but failed to return an indictment because of lack of evidence. Hall was subsequently indicted, but his trial resulted in a disagreement.

Tweed was indicted for felony. He remained at large on bail and was twice tried in 1873. The first trial resulted in a disagreement, the second in a conviction. His sentence was a fine of $12,000 and twelve years' imprisonment. When he arrived at the penitentiary, he answered the customary questions. "What occupation?" "Statesman." "What religion?" "None." He served one year and was then released on a flimsy technicality by the Court of Appeals. Civil suits were now brought, and, unable to obtain the $3,000,000 bail demanded, the fallen boss was sent to jail. He escaped to Cuba, and finally to Spain, but he was again arrested, returned to New York on a man-of-war, and put into Ludlow Street jail, where he died April 12, 1878, apparently without money or friends.

The exact amount of the plunder was never ascertained. An expert accountant employed by the housecleaners estimated that for three years, 1868–71, the frauds totaled between $45,000,000 and $50,000,000. The estimate of the aldermen's committee was $60,000,000. Tweed never gave any figures; he probably had never counted his gains, but merely spent them as they came. O'Rourke, one of the gang, estimated that the Ring stole about $75,000,000 during 1865–71, and that, "counting vast issues of fraudulent bonds," the looting "probably amounted to $200,000,000."

The story of these disclosures circled the earth and still affects the popular judgment of the American metropolis. It seemed as though Tammany were forever discredited. But, to the despair of reformers, in 1874 Tammany returned to power, electing its candidate for mayor by over 9000 majority. The new boss who maneuvered this rapid resurrection was John Kelly, a stone-mason, known among his Irish followers as "Honest

John." Besides the political probity which the
occasion demanded, he possessed a capacity for
knowing men and sensing public opinion. This
enabled him to lift the prostrate organization.
He persuaded such men as Samuel J. Tilden, the
distinguished lawyer, August Belmont, a leading
financier, Horatio Seymour, who had been governor, and Charles O'Conor, the famous advocate,
to become sachems under him. This was evidence of reform from within. Coöperation with
the Bar Association, the Taxpayers' Association,
and other similar organizations evidenced a desire of reform from without. Kelly "bossed" the
Hall until his death, June 1, 1886.

He was succeeded by Richard Croker, a machin-
ist, prize-fighter, and gang-leader. Croker began his official career as a court attendant under
the notorious Judge Barnard and later was an
engineer in the service of the city. These places
he held by Tammany favor, and he was so useful
that in 1868 he was made alderman. A quarrel
with Tweed lost him the place, but a reconcilia-
tion soon landed him in the lucrative office of
Superintendent of Market Fees and Rents, under
Connolly. In 1873 he was elected coroner and
ten years later was appointed fire commissioner.

6

His career as boss was marked by much political cleverness and caution and by an equal degree of moral obtuseness.

The triumph of Tammany in 1892 was followed by such ill-disguised corruption that the citizens of New York were again roused from their apathy. The investigations of the Fassett Committee of the State Senate two years previously had shown how deep the tentacles of Tammany were thrust into the administrative departments of the city. The Senate now appointed another investigating committee, of which Clarence Lexow was the chairman and John W. Goff the counsel. The Police Department came under its special scrutiny. The disclosures revealed the connivance of the police in stupendous election frauds. The President of the Police Board himself had distributed at the polls the policemen who committed these frauds. It was further revealed that vice and crime under police protection had been capitalized on a great scale. It was worth money to be a policeman. One police captain testified he had paid $15,000 for his promotions; another paid $12,000. It cost $300 to be appointed patrolman. Over six hundred policy-shops were open, each paying $1500 a month for protection; poolrooms paid $300 a month; bawdy-houses, from $25 to $50 per month per inmate. And their patrons paid whatever they could be blackmailed out of; streetwalkers, whatever they could be wheedled out of; saloons, $20 per month; pawnbrokers, thieves, and thugs shared with the police their profits, as did corporations and others seeking not only favors but their rights. The committee in its statement to the Grand Jury (March, 1892) estimated that the annual plunder from these sources was over $7,000,000.

During the committee's sessions Croker was in Europe on important business. But he found time to order the closing of disreputable resorts, and, though he was only a private citizen and three thousand miles away, his orders were promptly obeyed.

Aroused by these disclosures and stimulated by the lashing sermons of the Rev. Charles H. Parkhurst, the citizens of New York, in 1894, elected a reform government, with William L. Strong as Mayor. His administration set up for the metropolis a new standard of city management. Colonel George E. Waring organized, for the first time in the city's history, an efficient streetcleaning department. Theodore Roosevelt was appointed Police Commissioner. These men and their associates gave to New York a period of thrifty municipal housekeeping.

But the city returned to its filth. After the incorporation of Greater New York and the election of Robert A. Van Wyck as its mayor, the great beast of Tammany arose and extended its eager claws over the vast area of the new city.

The Mazet Committee was appointed by the legislature in 1899 to investigate rumors of renewed corruption. But the inquiry which followed was not as penetrating nor as free from partizan bias as thoughtful citizens wished. The principal exposure was of the Ice Trust, an attempt to monopolize the city's ice supply, in which city officials were stockholders, the mayor to the extent of 5000 shares, valued at $500,000. It was shown, too, that Tammany leaders were stockholders in corporations which received favors from the city. Governor Roosevelt, however, refused to remove Mayor Van Wyck because the evidence against him was insufficient.

The most significant testimony before the Mazet Committee was that given by Boss Croker himself. His last public office had been that of City Chamberlain, 1889–90, at a salary of $25,000. Two years later he purchased for $250,000 an interest in a stock-farm and paid over $100,000 for some noted race-horses. He spent over half a million dollars on the English race-track in three years and was reputed a million-aire, owning large blocks of city real estate. He told the committee that he virtually determined all city nominations; and that all candidates were assessed, even judicial candidates, from $10,000 to $25,000 for their nominations. "We try to have a pretty effective organization—that's what we are there for," he explained. "We are giving the people pure organization government," even though the organizing took "a lot of time" and was "very hard work." Tammany members stood by one another and helped each other, not only in politics but in business. "We want the whole business [city business] if we can get it." If "we win, we expect everyone to stand by us." Then he uttered what must have been to every citizen of understanding a self-evident truth, "I am working for my pockets all the time."

Soon afterwards Croker retired to his Irish castle, relinquishing the leadership to Charles Murphy, the present boss. The growing alertness of the voters, however, makes Murphy's task a more difficult one than that of any of his predecessors. It is doubtful if the nature of the machine has changed during all the years of its history. Tweed and Croker were only natural products of the system. They typify the vulgar climax of organized looting.

In 1913 the Independent Democrats, Republicans, and Progressives united in a fusion movement. They nominated and, after a most spirited campaign, elected John Purroy Mitchel as mayor. He was a young man, not yet forty, had held important city offices, and President Wilson had appointed him Collector of the Port of New York. His experience, his vigor, ability, and straight-dealing commended him to the friends of good government, and they were not disappointed. The Mitchel régime set a new record for clean and efficient municipal administration. Men of high character and ability were enlisted in public service, and the Police Department, under Commissioner Woods, achieved a new usefulness. The decent citizens, not alone in the metropolis, but throughout the country, believed with Theodore Roosevelt that Mr. Mitchel was "the best mayor New York ever had." But neither the effectiveness of his administration nor the combined efforts of the friends of good government could save him from the designs of Tammany Hall when, in 1917, he was a candidate for reëlection. Through a tactical blunder of the Fusionists, a small Republican group was permitted to control the party primaries and nominate a candidate of its own; the Socialists, greatly augmented by various pacifist groups, made heavy inroads among the foreign-born voters. And, while the whole power and finesse of Tammany were assiduously undermining the mayor's strength, ethnic, religious, partizan, and geographical prejudices combined to elect the machine candidate, Judge Hylan, a comparatively unknown Brooklyn magistrate.

How could Tammany regain its power, and that usually within two years, after such disclosures as we have seen? The main reason is the scientific efficiency of the organization. The victory of Burr in New York in 1800 was the first triumph of the first ward machine in America, and Tammany has forgotten neither this victory nor the methods by which it was achieved. The organization which was then set in motion has simply been enlarged to keep easy pace with the city's growth. There are, in fact, two organizations, Tammany Hall, the political machine, and Tammany Society, the "Columbian Order" organized by Mooney, which is ruled by sachems elected by the members. Both organizations, however, are one in spirit. We need concern ourselves only with the organization of Tammany Hall.

The framework of Tammany Hall's machinery has always been the general committee, still known, in the phraseology of Burr's day, as "the Democratic-Republican General Committee." It is a very democratic body composed of representatives from every assembly district, apportioned according to the number of voters in the district. The present apportionment is one committeeman for every fifteen votes. This makes a committee of over 9000, an unwieldy number. It is justified, however, on two very practical grounds: first, that it is large enough to keep close to the voters; and second, that its assessment of ten dollars a member brings in $90,000 a year to the war chest. This general committee holds stated meetings and appoints subcommittees. The executive committee, composed of the leaders of the assembly districts and the chairman

and treasurer of the county committee, is the
real working body of the great committee. It at-
tends to all important routine matters, selects candidates for office, and conducts their campaigns.
It is customary for the members of the general
committee to designate the district leaders for the
executive committee, but they are elected by their
own districts respectively at the annual primary
elections. The district leader is a very important
wheel in the machine. He not only leads his
district but represents it on the executive committee; and this brotherhood of leaders forms
the potent oligarchy of Tammany. Its sanction
crowns the high chieftain, the boss, who, in turn,
must be constantly on the alert that his throne is
not undermined; that is to say, he and his district
leaders must "play politics" within their own baili-
wicks to keep their heads on their own shoulders.
After their enfranchisement in New York (1917)
women were made eligible to the general and executive committees. Thirty-seven were at once
elected to the executive committee, and plans were
made to give them one-half of the representation
on the general committee.

Each of the twenty-three assembly districts is in
turn divided into election districts of about 400

voters, each with a precinct captain who is acquainted with every voter in his precinct and keeps track, as far as possible, of his affairs. In every assembly district there are headquarters and a club house, where the voters can go in the evening and enjoy a smoke, a bottle, and a more or less quiet game.

This organization is never dormant. And this is the key to its vitality. There is no mystery about it. Tammany is as vigilant between elections as it is on election day. It has always been solicitous for the poor and the humble, who most need and best appreciate help and attention. Every poor immigrant is welcomed, introduced to the district headquarters, given work, or food, or shelter. Tammany is his practical friend; and in return he is merely to become naturalized as quickly as possible under the wardship of a Tammany captain and by the grace of a Tammany judge, and then to vote the Tammany ticket. The new citizen's lessons in political science are all flavored with highly practical notions.

Tammany's machinery enables a house-to-house canvass to be made in one day. But this machinery must be oiled. There are three sources of the necessary lubricant: offices, jobs, the sale of favors; these are dependent on winning the elections. From its very earliest days, fraud at the polls has been a Tammany practice. As long as property qualifications were required, money was furnished for buying houses which could harbor a whole settlement of voters. It was not, however, until the adoption of universal suffrage that wholesale frauds became possible or useful; for with a limited suffrage it was necessary to sway only a few score votes to carry an ordinary election.

Fernando Wood set a new pace in this race for votes. It has been estimated that in 1854 there "were about 40,000 shiftless, unprincipled persons who lived by their wits and the labor of others. The trade of a part of these was turning primary elections, packing nominating conventions, repeating, and breaking up meetings." Wood also systematized naturalization. A card bearing the following legend was the open sesame to American citizenship:

"Common Pleas:
Please naturalize the bearer.
N. Seagrist, Chairman."

Seagrist was one of the men charged by an aldermanic committee "with robbing the funeral pall of

Henry Clay when his sacred person passed through this city."

When Hoffman was first elected mayor, over 15,000 persons were registered who could not be found at the places indicated. The naturalization machinery was then running at high speed. In 1868, from 25,000 to 30,000 foreigners were naturalized in New York in six weeks. Of 156,288 votes cast in the city, 25,000 were afterwards shown to be fraudulent. It was about this time that an official whose duty it was to swear in the election inspectors, not finding a Bible at hand, used a volume of Ollendorf's *New Method of Learning to Read, Write, and Speak French.* The courts sustained this substitution on the ground that it could not possibly have vitiated the election!

A new federal naturalization law and rigid election laws have made wholesale frauds impossible; and the genius of Tammany is now attempting to adjust itself to the new immigration, the new political spirit, and the new communal vigilance. Its power is believed by some optimistic observers to be waning. But the evidences are not wanting that its vitality and internal discipline are still persistent.

CHAPTER VI

LESSER OLIGARCHIES

New York City is not unique in its experience with political bossdom. Nearly every American city, in a greater or less degree, for longer or shorter periods, has been dominated by oligarchies.

Around Philadelphia, American sentiment has woven the memories of great events. It still remains, of all our large cities, the most "American." It has fewer aliens than any other, a larger percentage of home owners, a larger number of small tradespeople and skilled artisans — the sort of population which democracy exalts, and who in turn are presumed to be the bulwark of democracy. These good citizens, busied with the anxieties and excitements of their private concerns, discovered, in the decade following the Civil War, that their city had slipped unawares into the control of a compact oligarchy, the notorious Gas Ring.

The city government at this time was composed of thirty-two independent boards and departments, responsible to the council, but responsible to the council in name only and through the medium of a council committee. The coördinating force, the political gravitation which impelled all these diverse boards and council committees to act in unison, was the Gas Department. This department was controlled by a few designing and capable individuals under the captaincy of James McManes. They had reduced to political servitude all the employees of the department, numbering about two thousand. Then they had extended their sway over other city departments, especially the police department. Through the connivance of the police and control over the registration of voters, they soon dominated the primaries and the nominating conventions. They carried the banner of the Republican party, the dominant party in Philadelphia and in the State, under which they more easily controlled elections, for the people voted "regular." Then every one of the city's servants was made to pay to the Gas Ring money as well as obeisance. Tradespeople who sold supplies to the city, contractors who did its work, saloon-keepers and dive-owners who wanted protection — all paid. The city's debt increased at the rate of $3,000,000 a year, without visible evidence of the application of money to the city's growing needs.

In 1883 the citizens finally aroused themselves and petitioned the legislature for a new charter. They confessed: "Philadelphia is now recognized as the worst paved and worst cleaned city in the civilized world. The water supply is so bad that during many weeks of the last winter it was not only distasteful and unwholesome for drinking, but offensive for bathing purposes. The effort to clean the streets was abandoned for months and no attempt was made to that end until some public-spirited citizens, at their own expense, cleaned a number of the principal thoroughfares. . . . The physical condition of the sewers" is "dangerous to the health and most offensive to the comfort of our people. Public work has been done so badly that structures have to be renewed almost as soon as finished. Others have been in part constructed at enormous expense and then permitted to fall to decay without completion." This is a graphic and faithful description of the result which follows government of the Ring, for the Ring, with the people's money.

The legislature in 1885 granted Philadelphia a new charter, called the Bullitt Law, which went into effect in 1887, and which greatly simplified the structure of the government and centered responsibility in the mayor. It was then necessary for the Ring to control primaries and win elections in order to keep the city within its clutches. So began in Philadelphia the practice of fraudulent registering and voting on a scale that has probably never been equaled elsewhere in America. Names taken from tombstones in the cemeteries and from the register of births found their way to the polling registers. Dogs, cats, horses, anything living or dead, with a name, served the purpose.

The exposure of these frauds was undertaken in 1900 by the Municipal League. In two wards, where the population had decreased one per cent in ten years (1890–1900), it was found that the registered voters had increased one hundred per cent. From one house sixty-two voters were registered, of sundry occupations as follows: "Professors, bricklayers, gentlemen, moulders, cashiers, barbers, ministers, bakers, doctors, drivers, bartenders, plumbers, clerks, cooks, merchants, stevedores, bookkeepers, waiters, florists, boilermakers, salesmen, soldiers, electricians, printers, book agents, and restaurant keepers." One hundred and twenty-two voters, according to the register, lived at another house, including nine agents, nine machinists, nine gentlemen, nine waiters, nine salesmen, four barbers, four bakers, fourteen clerks, three laborers, two bartenders, a milkman, an optician, a piano-mover, a window-cleaner, a nurse, and so on.

On the day before the election the Municipal League sent registered letters to all the registered voters of certain precincts. Sixty-three per cent were returned, marked by the postman, "not at," "deceased," "removed," "not known." Of forty-four letters addressed to names registered from one four-story house, eighteen were returned. From another house, supposed to be sheltering forty-eight voters, forty-one were returned; from another, to which sixty-two were sent, sixty-one came back. The league reported that "two hundred and fifty-two votes were returned in a division that had less than one hundred legal voters within its boundaries." Repeating and ballot-box stuffing were common. Election officers would place fifty or more ballots in the box before the polls opened or would hand out a handful of ballots to the recognized repeaters.

The high-water mark of boss rule was reached under Mayor Ashbridge, "Stars-and-Stripes Sam," who had been elected in 1899. The moderation of Martin, who had succeeded McManes as boss, was cast aside; the mayor was himself a member of the Ring. When Ashbridge retired, the Municipal League reported: "The four years of the Ashbridge administration have passed into history leaving behind them a scar on the fame and reputation of our city which will be a long time healing. Never before, and let us hope never again, will there be such brazen defiance of public opinion, such flagrant disregard of public interest, such abuse of power and responsibility for private ends."

Since that time the fortunes of the Philadelphia Ring have fluctuated. Its hold upon the city, however, is not broken, but is still strong enough to justify Owen Wister's observation: "Not a Dickens, only a Zola, would have the face (and the stomach) to tell the whole truth about Philadelphia."

St. Louis was one of the first cities of America to possess the much-coveted home rule. The Missouri State Constitution of 1875 granted the

city the power to frame its own charter, under
certain limitations. The new charter provided for
a mayor elected for four years with the power of
appointing certain heads of departments; others,
however, were to be elected directly by the people.
It provided for a Municipal Assembly composed
of two houses: the Council, with thirteen members,
elected at large for four years, and the House of
Delegates, with twenty-eight members, one from
each ward, elected for two years. These two houses
were given coördinate powers; one was presumed
to be a check on the other. The Assembly fixed
the tax rate, granted franchises, and passed upon
all public improvements. The Police Department
was, however, under the control of the mayor
and four commissioners, the latter appointed by
the Governor. The city was usually Republican
by about 8000 majority; the State was safely
Democratic. The city, until a few years ago, had
few tenements and a small floating population.

Outwardly, all seemed well with the city until
1901, when the inside workings of its government were revealed to the public gaze through
the vengeance of a disappointed franchise-seeker.
The Suburban Railway Company sought an extension of its franchises. It had approached the

man known as the dispenser of such favors, but, thinking his price ($145,000) too high, had sought to deal directly with the Municipal Assembly. The price agreed upon for the House of Delegates was $75,000; for the Council, $60,000. These sums were placed in safety vaults controlled by a dual lock. The representative of the Company held one of the keys; the representative of the Assembly, the other; so that neither party could take the money without the presence of both. The Assembly duly granted the franchises; but property owners along the line of the proposed extension secured an injunction, which delayed the proceedings until the term of the venal House of Delegates had expired. The Assemblymen, having delivered the goods, demanded their pay. The Company, held up by the courts, refused. Mutterings of the disappointed conspirators reached the ear of an enterprising newspaper reporter. Thereby the Circuit Attorney, Joseph W. Folk, struck the trail of the gang. Both the president of the railway company and the "agent" of the rogues of the Assembly turned state's evidence; the safe-deposit boxes were opened, disclosing the packages containing one hundred and thirty-five $1000 bills.

This exposure led to others — the "Central Traction Conspiracy," the "Lighting Deal," the "Garbage Deal." In the cleaning-up process, thirty-nine persons were indicted, twenty-four for bribery and fifteen for perjury.

The evidence which Folk presented in the prosecution of these scoundrels merely confirmed what had long been an unsavory rumor: that franchises and contracts were bought and sold like merchandise; that the buyers were men of eminence in the city's business affairs; and that the sellers were the people's representatives in the Assembly. The Grand Jury reported: "Our investigation, covering more or less fully a period of ten years shows that, with few exceptions, no ordinance has been passed wherein valuable privileges or franchises are granted until those interested have paid the legislators the money demanded for action in the particular case. . . . So long has this practice existed that such members have come to regard the receipt of money for action on pending measures as a legitimate perquisite of a legislator."

These legislators, it appeared from the testimony, had formed a water-tight ring or "combine" in 1899, for the purpose of systematizing this traffic. A regular scale of prices was adopted: so much for an excavation, so much per foot for a railway switch, so much for a street pavement, so much for a grain elevator. Edward R. Butler was the master under whose commands for many years this trafficking was reduced to systematic perfection. He had come to St. Louis when a young man, had opened a blacksmith shop, had built up a good trade in horseshoeing, and also a pliant political following in his ward. His attempt to defeat the home rule charter in 1876 had given him wider prominence, and he soon became the boss of the Democratic machine. His energy, shrewdness, liberality, and capacity for friendship gave him sway over both Republican and Democratic votes in certain portions of the city. A prominent St. Louis attorney says that for over twenty years "he named candidates on both tickets, fixed, collected, and disbursed campaign assessments, determined the results in elections, and in fine, practically controlled the public affairs of St. Louis." He was the agent usually sought by franchise-seekers, and he said that had the Suburban Company dealt with him instead of with the members of the Assembly, they might have avoided exposure. He was indicted four times in the upheaval, twice for attempting to bribe the Board of Health in the garbage deal — he was a stockholder in the company seeking the contract — and twice for bribery in the lighting contract.

Cincinnati inherited from the Civil War the domestic excitements and political antagonisms of a border city. Its large German population gave it a conservative political demeanor, slow to accept changes, loyal to the Republican party as it was to the Union. This reduced partizan opposition to a docile minority, willing to dicker for public spoils with the intrenched majority.

George B. Cox was for thirty years the boss of this city. Events had prepared the way for him. Following closely upon the war, Tom Campbell, a crafty criminal lawyer, was the local leader of the Republicans, and John R. McLean, owner of the Cincinnati *Enquirer*, a very rich man, of the Democrats. These two men were cronies: they bartered the votes of their followers. For some years crime ran its repulsive course: brawlers, thieves, cut-throats escaped conviction through the defensive influence of the lawyer-boss. In 1880, Cox, who had served an apprenticeship in his brother-in-law's gambling house, was elected to the city council. Thence he was promoted to the decennial board of equalization which appraised all real estate every ten years. There followed a great decrease in the valuation of some of the choicest holdings in the city. In 1884 there were riots in Cincinnati. After the acquittal of two brutes who had murdered a man for a trifling sum of money, exasperated citizens burned the criminal court house. The barter in justice stopped, but the barter in offices and in votes continued. The Blaine campaign then in progress was in great danger. Cox, already a master of the political game, promised the Republican leaders that if they would give him a campaign fund he would turn in a Republican majority from Cincinnati. He did; and for many years thereafter the returns from Hamilton County, in which Cincinnati is situated, brought cheer to Republican State headquarters on election night.

Cox was an unostentatious, silent man, giving one the impression of sullenness, and almost entirely lacking in those qualities of comradeship which one usually seeks in the "Boss" type. From a barren little room over the "Mecca" saloon, with the help of a telephone, he managed his machine. He never obtruded himself upon the public. He always remained in the background. Nor did he ever take vast sums. Moderation was the rule of his loot.

By 1905 a movement set in to rid the city of machine rule. Cox saw this movement growing in strength. So he imported boatloads of floaters from Kentucky. These floaters registered "from dives, and doggeries, from coal bins and water closets; no space was too small to harbor a man." For once he threw prudence to the winds. Exposure followed; over 2800 illegal voters were found. The newspapers, so long docile, now provided the necessary publicity. A little paper, the *Citizen's Bulletin*, which had started as a handbill of reform, when all the dailies seemed closed to the facts, now grew into a sturdy weekly. And, to add the capstone to Cox's undoing, William H. Taft, the most distinguished son of Cincinnati, then Secretary of War in President Roosevelt's cabinet, in a campaign speech in Akron, Ohio, advised the Republicans to repudiate him. This confounded the "regulars," and Cox was partially beaten. The reformers elected their candidate for mayor, but the boss retained his hold on the county and the city council. And, in spite of all that was done, Cox remained an influence in politics until his death, May 20, 1916.

San Francisco has had a varied and impressive political experience. The first legislature of California incorporated the mining town into the city of San Francisco, April 15, 1850. Its government from the outset was corrupt and inefficient. Lawlessness culminated in the murder of the editor of the *Bulletin*, J. King of William, on May 14, 1856, and a vigilance committee was organized to clean up the city, and watch the ballot-box on election day.

Soon the legislature was petitioned to change the charter. The petition recites: "Without a change in the city government which shall diminish the weight of taxation, the city will neither be able to discharge the interest on debts already contracted, nor to meet the demands for current disbursements. . . . The present condition of the streets and public improvements of the city abundantly attest the total inefficiency of the present system."

The legislature passed the "Consolidation Act," and from 1856 to 1900 county and city were governed as a political unit. At first the hopes for more frugal government seemed to be fulfilled. But all encouraging symptoms soon vanished. Partizan rule followed, encouraged by the tinkering of the legislature, which imposed on the charter layer upon layer of amendments, dictated by partizan craft, not by local needs. The administrative departments were managed by Boards of Commissioners, under the dictation of "Blind Boss Buckley," who governed his kingdom for many years with the despotic benevolence characteristic of his kind. The citizens saw their money squandered and their public improvements lagging. It took twenty-five years to complete the City Hall, at a cost of $5,500,000. An official of the Citizens' Non-partizan party, in 1895, said: "There is no city in the Union with a quarter of a million people, which would not be the better for a little judicious hanging."

The repeated attempts made by citizens of San Francisco to get a new charter finally succeeded, and in 1900 the city hopefully entered a new epoch under a charter of its own making which contained several radical changes. Executive responsibility was centered in the mayor, fortified by a comprehensive civil service. The foundations were laid for municipal ownership of public utilities, and the initiative and referendum were adopted for all public franchises. The legislative power was vested in a board of eighteen supervisors elected at large.

No other American city so dramatically represents the futility of basing political optimism on a mere plan. It was only a step from the mediocrity enthroned by the first election under the new charter to the gross inefficiency and corruption of a new ring, under a new boss. A Grand Jury (called the "Andrews Jury") made a report indicating that the administration was trafficking in favors sold to gamblers, prize-fighters, criminals, and the whole gamut of the underworld; that illegal profits were being reaped from illegal contracts, and that every branch of the executive department was honeycombed with corruption. The Grand Jury believed and said all this, but it lacked the legal proof upon which Mayor Schmitz and his accomplices could be indicted. In spite of this report, Schmitz was reëlected in 1905 as the candidate of the Labor-Union party.

Now graft in San Francisco became simply universal. George Kennan, summarizing the practices of the looters, says they "took toll everywhere from everybody and in almost every imaginable way: they went into partnership with dishonest contractors; sold privileges and permits to business men: extorted money from restaurants and saloons; levied assessments on municipal employees; shared the profits of houses of prostitution; forced beer, whiskey, champagne, and cigars on restaurants and saloons on commission; blackmailed gamblers, pool-sellers, and promoters of prize-fights; sold franchises to wealthy corporations; created such municipal bureaus as the commissary department and the city commercial company in order to make robbery of the city more easy; leased rooms and buildings for municipal offices at exorbitant rates, and compelled the lessees to share profits; held up milkmen, kite-advertisers, junk-dealers, and even street-sweepers; and took bribes from everybody who wanted an illegal privilege and was willing to pay for it. The motto of the administration seemed to be 'Encourage dishonesty, and then let no dishonest dollar escape.'"

The machinery through which this was effected was simple: the mayor had vast appointing powers and by this means directly controlled all the city departments. But the mayor was only an automaton. Back of him was Abe Ruef, the Boss, an unscrupulous lawyer who had wormed his way into the labor party, and manipulated the "leaders" like puppets. Ruef's game also was elementary. He sold his omnipotence for cash, either under the respectable cloak of "retainer" or under the more common device of commissions and dividends, so that thugs retained him for their freedom, contractors for the favors they expected, and public service corporations for their franchises.

Finally, through the persistence of a few private citizens, a Grand Jury was summoned. Under the foremanship of B. P. Oliver it made a thorough investigation. Francis J. Heney was employed as special prosecutor and William J. Burns as detective. Heney and Burns formed an aggressive team. The Ring proved as vulnerable as it was rotten. Over three hundred indictments were returned, involving persons in every walk of life. Ruef was sentenced to fourteen years in the penitentiary. Schmitz was freed on a technicality, after being found guilty and sentenced to five years. Most of the other indictments were not tried, the prosecutor's attention having been diverted to the trail of the franchise-seekers, who have thus far eluded conviction.

Minneapolis, a city blending New England traditions with Scandinavian thrift, illustrates, in its experiences with "Doc" Ames, the maneuvers of the peripatetic boss. Ames was four times mayor of the city, but never his own successor. Each succeeding experience with him grew more lurid of indecency, until his third term was crystallized in Minneapolis tradition as "the notorious Ames administration." Domestic scandal made him a social outcast, political corruption a byword, and Ames disappeared from public view for ten years.

In 1900 a new primary law provided the opportunity to return him to power for the fourth time. Ames, who had been a Democrat, now found it convenient to become a Republican. The new law, like most of the early primary laws, permitted members of one party to vote in the primaries of the other party. So Ames's following, estimated at about fifteen hundred, voted in the Republican primaries, and he became a regular candidate of that party in a presidential year, when citizens felt the special urge to vote for the party.

Ames was the type of boss with whom discipline is secondary to personal aggrandizement. He had a passion for popularity; was imposing of presence; possessed considerable professional skill; and played constantly for the support of the poor. The attacks upon him he turned into political capital by saying that he was made a victim by the rich because he championed the poor. Susceptible to flattery and fond of display, he lacked the power to command. He had followers, not henchmen. His following was composed of the lowly, who were duped by his phrases, and of criminals, who knew his bent; and they followed him into any party whither he found it convenient to go, Republican, Democratic, or Populist.

The charter of Minneapolis gave the mayor considerable appointing power. He was virtually the dictator of the Police Department. This was the great opportunity of Ames and his floating vote. His own brother, a weak individual with a dubious record, was made Chief of Police. Within a few weeks about one-half of the police force was discharged, and the places filled with men who could be trusted by the gang. The number of detectives was increased and an ex-gambler placed at their head. A medical student from Ames's office was commissioned a special policeman to gather loot from the women of the street.

Through a telepathy of their own, the criminal

classes all over the country soon learned of the favorable conditions in Minneapolis, under which every form of gambling and low vice flourished; and burglars, pickpockets, safe-blowers, and harlots made their way thither. Mr. W. A. Frisbie, the editor of a leading Minneapolis paper, described the situation in the following words: "It is no exaggeration to say that in this period fully 99% of the police department's efficiency was devoted to the devising and enforcing of blackmail. Ordinary patrolmen on beats feared to arrest known criminals for fear the prisoners would prove to be 'protected.' . . . The horde of detective favorites hung lazily about police headquarters, waiting for some citizen to make complaint of property stolen, only that they might enforce additional blackmail against the thief, or possibly secure the booty for themselves. One detective is now [1903] serving time in the state prison for retaining a stolen diamond pin."

The mayor thought he had a machine for grinding blackmail from every criminal operation in his city, but he had only a gang, without discipline or coördinating power, and weakened by jealousy and suspicion. The wonder is that it lasted fifteen months. Then came the "April Grand Jury," under the foremanship of a courageous and resourceful business man. The régime of criminals crumbled; forty-nine indictments, involving twelve persons, were returned.

The Grand Jury, however, at first stood alone in its investigations. The crowd of politicians and vultures were against it, and no appropriations were granted for getting evidence. So its members paid expenses out of their own pockets, and its foreman himself interviewed prisoners and discovered the trail that led to the Ring's undoing. Ames's brother was convicted on second trial and sentenced to six and a half years in the penitentiary, while two of his accomplices received shorter terms. Mayor Ames, under indictment and heavy bonds, fled to Indiana.

The President of the City Council, a business man of education, tact, and sincerity, became mayor, for an interim of four months; enough time, as it proved, for him to return the city to its normal political life.

These examples are sufficient to illustrate the organization and working of the municipal machine. It must not be imagined by the reader that these cities alone, and a few others made notorious by the magazine muck-rakers, are the only American cities that have developed oligarchies. In truth, not a single American city, great or small, has entirely escaped, for a greater or lesser period, the sway of a coterie of politicians. It has not always been a corrupt sway; but it has rarely, if ever, given efficient administration.

Happily there are not wanting signs that the general conditions which have fostered the Ring are disappearing. The period of reform set in about 1890, when people began to be interested in the study of municipal government. It was not long afterwards that the first authoritative books on the subject appeared. Then colleges began to give courses in municipal government; editors began to realize the public's concern in local questions and to discuss neighborhood politics as well as national politics. By 1900 a new era broke — the era of the Grand Jury. Nothing so hopeful in local politics had occurred in our history as the disclosures which followed. They provoked the residuum of conscience in the citizenry and the determination that honesty should rule in public business and politics as well as in private transactions. The Grand Jury inquisitions, however, demonstrated clearly that the criminal law was no remedy for municipal mis-rule. The great majority of floaters and illegal voters who were indicted never faced a trial jury. The results of the prosecutions for bribery and grosser political crimes were scarcely more encour-aging. It is true that one Abe Ruef in a California penitentiary is worth untold sermons, editorials, and platform admonitions, and serves as a potent warning to all public malefactors. Yet the ex-ample is soon forgotten; and the people return to their former political habits.

But out of this decade of gang-hunting and its impressive experiences with the shortcomings of our criminal laws came the new municipal era which we have now fully entered, the era of enlight-ened administration. This new era calls for a reconstruction of the city government. Its princi-pal feature is the rapid spread of the Galveston or Commission form of government and of its modi-fication, the City Manager plan, the aim of which is to centralize governmental authority and to entice able men into municipal office. And there are many other manifestations of the new civic spirit. The mesmeric influence of national party names in civic politics is waning; the rise of home rule for the city is severing the unholy alliance between the legislature and the local Ring; the power to grant franchises is being taken away from legislative bodies and placed directly with the people; nominations are passing out of the hands of cliques and are being made the gift of the voters through petitions and primaries; efficient reforms in the taxing and budgetary machinery have been instituted, and the development of the merit system in the civil service is creating a class of municipal experts beyond the reach of political gangsters.

There have sprung up all sorts of collateral organizations to help the officials: societies for municipal research, municipal reference libraries, citizens' unions, municipal leagues, and municipal parties. These are further supplemented by organizations which indirectly add to the momentum of practical, enlightened municipal sentiment: boards of commerce, associations of business and professional men of every variety, women's clubs, men's clubs, children's clubs, recreation clubs, social clubs, every one with its own peculiar vigilance upon some corner of the city's affairs. So every important city is guarded by a network of voluntary organizations.

All these changes in city government, in munici-

pal laws and political mechanisms, and in the
people's attitude toward their cities, have tended
to dignify municipal service. The city job has
been lifted to a higher plane. Lord Rosebery,
the brilliant chairman of the first London County
Council, the governing body of the world's largest
city, said many years ago: "I wish that my voice
could extend to every municipality in the kingdom, and impress upon every man, however high
his position, however great his wealth, however
consummate his talents may be, the importance
and nobility of municipal work." It is such a
spirit as this that has made the government of
Glasgow a model of democratic efficiency; and it
is the beginnings of this spirit that the municipal
historian finds developing in the last twenty years
of American life. It is indeed difficult to see how
our cities can slip back again into the clutches of
bosses and rings and repeat the shameful history
of the last decades of the nineteenth century.

CHAPTER VII

LEGISLATIVE OMNIPOTENCE

THE American people, when they wrote their first state constitutions, were filled with a profound distrust of executive authority, the offspring of their experience with the arbitrary King George. So they saw to it that the executive authority in their own government was reduced to its lowest terms, and that the legislative authority, which was presumed to represent the people, was exalted to legal omnipotence. In the original States, the legislature appointed many of the judicial and administrative officers; it was above the executive veto; it had political supremacy; it determined the form of local governments and divided the State into election precincts; it appointed the delegates to the Continental Congress, towards which it displayed the attitude of a sovereign. It was altogether the most important arm of the state government; in fact it virtually *was* the state government.

The Federal Constitution created a government of specified powers, reserving to the States all authority not expressly given to the central government. Congress can legislate only on subjects permitted by the Constitution; on the other hand, a state legislature can legislate on any subject not expressly forbidden. The state legislature possesses authority over a far wider range of subjects than Congress — subjects, moreover, which press much nearer to the daily activities of the citizens, such as the wide realm of private law, personal relations, local government, and property.

In the earlier days, men of first-class ability, such as Alexander Hamilton, Samuel Adams, and James Madison, did not disdain membership in the state legislatures. But the development of party spirit and machine politics brought with it a great change. Then came the legislative caucus; and party politics soon reigned in every capital. As the legislature was ruled by the majority, the dominant party elected presiding officers, designated committees, appointed subordinates, and controlled lawmaking. The party was therefore in a position to pay its political debts and bestow upon its supporters valuable favors. Further, as the legislature apportioned the various electoral districts, the dominant party could, by means of the gerrymander, entrench itself even in unfriendly localities. And, to crown its political power, it elected United States Senators. But, as the power of the party increased, unfortunately the personnel of the legislature deteriorated. Able men, as a rule, shunned a service that not only took them from their private affairs for a number of months, but also involved them in partizan rivalries and trickeries. Gradually the people came to lose confidence in the legislative body and to put their trust more in the Executive or else reserved governmental powers to themselves. It was about 1835 that the decline of the legislature's powers set in, when new state constitutions began to clip its prerogatives, one after another.

The bulky constitutions now adopted by most of the States are eloquent testimony to the complete collapse of the legislature as an administrative body and to the people's general distrust of their chosen representatives. The initiative, referendum, recall, and the withholding of important subjects from the legislature's power, are among the devices intended to free the people from the machinations of their wilful representatives.

Now, most of the evils which these heroic measures have sought to remedy can be traced directly to the partizan ownership of the state legislature. The boss controlling the members of the legislature could not only dole out his favors to the privilege seekers; he could assuage the greed of the municipal ring; and could, to a lesser degree, command federal patronage by an *entente cordiale* with congressmen and senators; and through his power in presidential conventions and elections he had a direct connection with the presidential office itself.

It was in the days before the legislature was prohibited from granting, by special act, franchises and charters, when banks, turnpike companies, railroads, and all sorts of corporations came asking for charters, that the figure of the lobbyist first appeared. He acted as a middleman between the seeker and the giver. The preëminent figure of this type in state and legislative politics for several decades preceding the Civil War was Thurlow Weed of New York. As an influencer of legislatures, he stands easily first in ability and achievement. His great personal attractions won him willing followers whom he knew how to use. He was party manager, as well as lobbyist and boss in a real sense long before that term was coined.

His capacity for politics amounted to genius. He never sought office; and his memory has been left singularly free from taint. He became the editor of the Albany *Journal* and made it the leading Whig "up-state" paper. His friend Seward, whom he had lifted into the Governor's chair, passed on to the United States Senate; and when Horace Greeley with the New York *Tribune* joined their forces, this potent triumvirate ruled the Empire State. Greeley was its spokesman, Seward its leader, but Weed was its designer. From his room No. 11 in the old Astor House, he beckoned to forces that made or unmade presidents, governors, ambassadors, congressmen, judges, and legislators.

With the tremendous increase of business after the Civil War, New York City became the central office of the nation's business, and many of the interests centered there found it wise to have permanent representatives at Albany to scrutinize every bill that even remotely touched their welfare, to promote legislation that was frankly in their favor, and to prevent "strikes" — the bills designed for blackmail. After a time, however, the number of "strikes" decreased, as well as the number of lobbyists attending the session. The corporate interests had learned efficiency. Instead of dealing with legislators individually, they arranged with the boss the price of peace or of desirable legislation. The boss transmitted his wishes to his puppets. This form of government depends upon a machine that controls the legislature. In New York both parties were moved by machines. "Tom" Platt was the "easy boss" of the Republicans; and Tammany and its "up-state" affiliations controlled the Democrats. "Right here," says Platt in his *Autobiography* (1910), "it may be appropriate to say that I have had more or less to do with the organization of the New York legislature since 1873." He had. For forty years he practically named the Speaker and committees when his party won, and he named the price when his party lost. All that an "interest" had to do, under the new plan, was to "see the boss," and the powers of government were delivered into its lap.

Some of this legislative bargaining was revealed in the insurance investigation of 1905, conducted by the Armstrong Committee with Charles E. Hughes as counsel. Officers of the New York Life Insurance Company testified that their company had given $50,000 to the Republican campaign of

1904. An item of $235,000, innocently charged to "Home office annex account," was traced to the hands of a notorious lobbyist at Albany. Three insurance companies had paid regularly $50,000 each to the Republican campaign fund. Boss Platt himself was compelled reluctantly to relate how he had for fifteen years received ten one thousand dollar bundles of greenbacks from the Equitable Life as "consideration" for party goods delivered. John A. McCall, President of the New York Life, said: "I don't care about the Republican side of it or the Democratic side of it. It doesn't count at all with me. What is best for the New York Life moves and actuates me."

In another investigation Mr. H. O. Havemeyer of the Sugar Trust said: "We have large interests in this State; we need police protection and fire protection; we need everything that the city furnishes and gives, and we have to support these things. Every individual and corporation and firm —trust or whatever you call it—does these things and we do them." No distinction is made, then, between the government that ought to furnish this "protection" and the machine that sells it!

No episode in recent political history shows better the relations of the legislature to the political machine and the great power of invisible government than the impeachment and removal of Governor William Sulzer in 1913. Sulzer had been four times elected to the legislature. He served as Speaker in 1893. He was sent to Congress by an East Side district in New York City in 1895 and served continuously until his nomination for Governor of New York in 1912. All these years he was known as a Tammany man. During his campaign for Governor he made many promises for reform, and after his election he issued a bombastic declaration of independence. His words were discounted in the light of his previous record. Immediately after his inauguration, however, he began a house-cleaning. He set to work an economy and efficiency commission; he removed a Tammany superintendent of prisons; made unusually good appointments without paying any attention to the machine; and urged upon the legislature vigorous and vital laws.

But the Tammany party had a large working majority in both houses, and the changed Sulzer was given no support. The crucial moment came when an emasculated primary law was handed to him for his signature. An effective primary law had been a leading campaign issue, all the parties being pledged to such an enactment. The one which the Governor was now requested to sign had been framed by the machine to suit its pleasure. The Governor vetoed it. The legislature adjourned on the 3rd of May. The Governor promptly reconvened it in extra session (June 7th) for the purpose of passing an adequate primary law. Threats that had been made against him by the machine now took form. An investigating committee, appointed by the Senate to examine the Governor's record, largely by chance happened upon "pay dirt," and early on the morning of the 13th of August, after an all-night session, the Assembly passed a motion made by its Tammany floor leader to impeach the Governor.

The articles of impeachment charged: first, that the Governor had filed a false report of his campaign expenses; second, that since he had made such statement under oath he was guilty of perjury; third, that he had bribed witnesses to withhold testimony from the investigating committee; fourth, that he had used threats in suppression of evidence before the same tribunal; fifth, that he had persuaded a witness from responding to the committee's subpoena; sixth, that he had used campaign contributions for private speculation in the stock market; seventh, that he had used his power as Governor to influence the political action of certain officials; lastly, that he had used this power for affecting the stock market to his gain.

Unfortunately for the Governor, the first, second, and sixth charges had a background of facts, although the rest were ridiculous and trivial. By a vote of 43 to 12 he was removed from the governorship. The proceeding was not merely an impeachment of New York's Governor. It was an impeachment of its government. Every citizen knew that if Sulzer had obeyed Murphy, his shortcomings would never have been his undoing.

The great commonwealth of Pennsylvania was for sixty years under the domination of the House of Cameron and the House of Quay. Simon Cameron's entry into public notoriety was symbolic of his whole career. In 1838, he was one of a commission of two to disburse to the Winnebago Indians at Prairie du Chien $100,000 in gold. But, instead of receiving gold, the poor Indians received only a few thousand dollars in the notes of a bank of which Cameron was the cashier.

Cameron was for this reason called "the Great Winnebago." He built a large fortune by canal and railway contracts, and later by rolling-mills and furnaces. He was one of the first men in American politics to purchase political power by the lavish use of cash, and to use political power for the gratification of financial greed. In 1857 he was elected to the United States Senate as a Republican by a legislature in which the Democrats had a majority. Three Democrats voted for him, and so bitter was the feeling against the renegade trio that no hotel in Harrisburg would shelter them.

In 1860 he was a candidate for the Republican presidential nomination. President Lincoln made him Secretary of War. But his management was so ill-savored that a committee of leading business men from the largest cities of the country told the President that it was impossible to transact business with such a man. These complaints coupled with other considerations moved Lincoln to dismiss Cameron. He did so in characteristic fashion. On January 11, 1862, he sent Cameron a curt note saying that he proposed to appoint him minister to Russia. And thither into exile Cameron went. A few months later, the House of

Representatives passed a resolution of censure, citing Cameron's employment of irresponsible persons and his purchase of supplies by private contract instead of competitive bidding. The resolution, however, was later expunged from the records; and Cameron, on his return from Russia, again entered the Senate under circumstances so suspicious that only the political influence of the boss thwarted an action for bribery. In 1877 he resigned, naming as his successor his son "Don," who was promptly elected.

In the meantime another personage had appeared on the scene. "Cameron made the use of money an essential to success in politics, but Quay made politics expensive beyond the most extravagant dreams." From the time he arrived of age until his death, with the exception of three or four years, Matthew S. Quay held public office. When the Civil War broke out, he had been for some time prothonotary of Beaver County, and during the war he served as Governor Curtin's private secretary. In 1865 he was elected to the legislature. In 1877 he induced the legislature to resurrect the discarded office of Recorder of Philadelphia, and for two years he collected the annual fees of $40,000. In 1887 he was elected to the United States Senate, in which he remained except for a brief interval until his death.

In 1899 came revelations of Quay's substantial interests in state moneys. The suicide of the cashier of the People's Bank of Philadelphia, which was largely owned by politicians and was a favorite depository of state funds, led to an investigation of the bank's affairs, and disclosed the fact that Quay and some of his associates had used state funds for speculation. Quay's famous telegram to the cashier was found among the dead official's papers, "If you can buy and carry a thousand Met. for me I will shake the plum tree."

Quay was indicted, but escaped trial by pleading the statute of limitations as preventing the introduction of necessary evidence against him. A great crowd of shouting henchmen accosted him as a hero when he left the court-room, and escorted him to his hotel. And the legislature soon thereafter elected him to his third term in the Senate.

Pittsburg, as well as Philadelphia, had its machine which was carefully geared to Quay's state machine. The connection was made clear by the testimony of William Flinn, a contractor boss, before a committee of the United States Senate.

Flinn explained the reason for a written agreement between Quay on the one hand and Flinn and one Brown in behalf of Chris Magee, the Big Boss, on the other, for the division of the sovereignty of western Pennsylvania. "Senator Quay told me," said Flinn, "that he would not permit us to elect the Republican candidate for mayor in Pittsburg unless we adjust the politics to suit him." The people evidently had nothing to say about it.

The experiences of New York and Pennsylvania are by no means isolated; they are illustrative. Very few States have escaped a legislative scandal. In particular, Rhode Island, Delaware, Illinois, Colorado, Montana, California, Ohio, Mississippi, Texas can give pertinent testimony to the willingness of legislatures to prostitute their great powers to the will of the boss or the machine.

CHAPTER VIII

THE NATIONAL HIERARCHY

AMERICAN political maneuver culminates at Washington. The Presidency and membership in the Senate and the House of Representatives are the great stakes. By a venerable tradition, scrupulously followed, the judicial department is kept beyond the reach of party greed.

The framers of the Constitution believed that they had contrived a method of electing the President and Vice-President which would preserve the choice from partizan taint. Each State should choose a number of electors "equal to the whole number of Senators and Representatives to which the State may be entitled in the Congress." These electors were to form an independent body, to meet in their respective States and "ballot for two persons," and send the result of their balloting to the Capitol, where the President of the Senate, in the presence of the Senate and the House of Representatives, opened the certificates and counted the votes. The one receiving the greatest number of votes was to be declared elected President, the one receiving the next highest number of votes, Vice-President. George Washington was the only President elected by such an autonomous group. The election of John Adams was bitterly contested, and the voters knew, when they were casting their ballots in 1796, whether they were voting for a Federalist or a Jeffersonian. From that day forward this greatest of political prizes has been awarded through partizan competition. In 1804 the method of selecting the Vice-President was changed by the twelfth constitutional amendment. The electors since that time ballot for President and Vice-President. Whatever may be the legal privileges of the members of the Electoral College, they are considered, by the voters, as agents of the party upon whose tickets their names appear, and to abuse this relationship would universally be deemed an act of perfidy.

The Constitution permits the legislatures of the States to determine how the electors shall be chosen. In the earlier period, the legislatures elected them; later they were elected by the people; sometimes they were elected at large, but usually they were chosen by districts. And this is now the general custom. Since the development of direct nominations, there has been a strong movement towards the abolition of the Electoral College and the election of the President by direct vote.

The President is the most powerful official in our government and in many respects he is the most powerful ruler in the world. He is Commander-in-Chief of the Army and Navy. His is virtually the sole responsibility in conducting international relations. He is at the head of the civil administration and all the important administrative departments are answerable to him. He possesses a vast power of appointment through which he dispenses political favors. His wish is potent in shaping legislation and his veto is rarely overridden. With Congress he must be in daily contact; for the Senate has the power of ratifying or discarding his appointments and of sanctioning or rejecting his treaties with foreign countries; and the House of Representatives originates all money bills and thus possesses a formidable check upon executive usurpation.

The Constitution originally reposed the choice of United States Senators with the state legislatures. A great deal of virtue was to flow from such an indirect election. The members of the legislature were presumed to act with calm judgment and to choose only the wise and experienced for the dignity of the toga. And until the period following the Civil War the great majority of the States delighted to send their ablest statesmen to the Senate. Upon its roll we find the names of many of our illustrious orators and jurists. After the Civil War, when the spirit of commercialism invaded every activity, men who were merely rich began to aspire to senatorial honors. The debauch of the state legislatures which was revealed in the closing year of the nineteenth century and the opening days of the twentieth so revolted the people that the seventeenth constitutional amendment was adopted (1913) providing for the election of senators by direct vote.

The House of Representatives was designed to be the "popular house." Its election from small districts, by direct vote, every two years is a guarantee of its popular character. From this characteristic it has never departed. It is the People's House. It originates all revenue measures. On its floor, in the rough and tumble of debate, partizan motives are rarely absent.

Upon this national tripod, the Presidency, the

Senate, and the House, is builded the vast national party machine. Every citizen is familiar with the outer aspect of these great national parties as they strive in placid times to create a real issue of the tariff, or imperialism, or what not, so as to establish at least an ostensible difference between them; or as they, in critical times, make the party name synonymous with national security. The high-sounding platforms, the frenzied orators, the parades, mass-meetings, special trains, pamphlets, books, editorials, lithographs, posters — all these paraphernalia are conjured up in the voter's mind when he reads the words Democratic and Republican.

But, from the standpoint of the professional politician, all this that the voter sees is a mask, the patriotic veneer to hide the machine, that complex hierarchy of committees ranging from Washington to every cross-roads in the Republic. The committee system, described in a former chapter, was perfected by the Republican party during the days of the Civil War, under the stress of national necessity. The great party leaders were then in Congress. When the assassination of Lincoln placed Andrew Johnson in power, the bitter quarrel between Congress and the President firmly united the Republicans; and in order to carry the mid-election in 1866, they organized a Congressional Campaign Committee to conduct the canvass. This practice has been continued by both parties, and in "off" years it plays a very prominent part in the party campaign. Congress alone, however, was only half the conquest. It was only through control of the Administration that access was gained to the succulent herbage of federal pasturage and that vast political prestige with the voter was achieved.

The President is nominally the head of his party. In reality he may not be; he may be only the President. That depends upon his personality, his desires, his hold upon Congress and upon the people, and upon the circumstances of the hour. During the Grant Administration, as already described, there existed, in every sense of the term, a federal machine. It held Congress, the Executive, and the vast federal patronage in its power. All the federal office-holders, all the postmasters and their assistants, revenue collectors, inspectors, clerks, marshals, deputies, consuls, and ambassadors were a part of the organization, contributing to its maintenance. We often hear today of the "Federal Crowd," a term used to describe such appointees as still subsist on presidential and senatorial favor. In Grant's time, this "crowd" was a genuine machine, constructed, unlike some of its successors, from the center outward. But the "boss" of this machine was not the President. It was controlled by a group of leading Congressmen, who used their power for dictating appointments and framing "desirable" legislation. Grant, in the imagination of the people, symbolized the cause their sacrifices had won; and thus his moral prestige became the cloak of the political plotters.

A number of the ablest men in the Republican party, however, stood aloof; and by 1876 a movement against the manipulators had set in. Civil service reform had become a real issue. Hayes, the "dark horse" who was nominated in that year, declared, in accepting the nomination, that "reform should be thorough, radical, and complete." He promised not to be a candidate for a second term, thus avoiding the temptation, to which almost every President has succumbed, of using the patronage to secure his reëlection. The party managers pretended not to hear these promises. And when Hayes, after his inauguration, actually began to put them into force, they set the whole machinery of the party against the President.   Matters came to a head when the President issued an order commanding federal office-holders to refrain from political activity. This order was generally defied, especially in New York City in the post-office and customs rings. Two notorious offenders, Cornell and Arthur, were dismissed from office by the President.   But the Senate, influenced by Roscoe Conkling's power, refused to confirm the President's new appointees; and under the Tenure of Office Act, which had been passed to tie President Johnson's hands, the offenders remained in office over a year.   The fight disciplined the President and the machine in about equal proportions.   The President became more amenable and the machine less arbitrary.

President Garfield attempted the impossible feat of obliging both the politicians and the reformers.   He was persuaded to make nominations to federal offices in New York without consulting either of the senators from that State, Conkling and Platt.   Conkling appealed to the Senate to reject the New York appointees sent in by the President.   The Senate failed to sustain him. Conkling and his colleague Platt resigned from the Senate and appealed to the New York legislature, which also refused to sustain them.

While this absurd farce was going on, a more serious ferment was brewing. On July 2, 1881, President Garfield was assassinated by a disappointed office-seeker named Guiteau. The attention of the people was suddenly turned from the ridiculous diversion of the Conkling incident to the tragedy and its cause. They saw the chief office in their gift a mere pawn in the game of place-seekers, the time and energy of their President wasted in bickerings with congressmen over petty appointments, and the machinery of their Government dominated by the machinery of the party for ignoble or selfish ends.

At last the advocates of reform found their opportunity. In 1883 the Civil Service Act was passed, taking from the President about 14,000 appointments. Since then nearly every President, towards the end of his term, especially his second term, has added to the numbers, until nearly two-thirds of the federal offices are now filled by examination. President Cleveland during his second term made sweeping additions. President Roosevelt found about 100,000 in the classified service and left 200,000. President Taft, before his retirement, placed in the classified service assistant postmasters and clerks in first- and second-class post-offices, about 42,000 rural delivery carriers, and over 20,000 skilled workers in the navy yards.

The appointing power of the President, however, still remains the principal point of his contact with the machine. He has, of course, other means of showing partizan favors. Tariff laws, laws regulating interstate commerce, reciprocity treaties, "pork barrels," pensions, financial policies, are all pregnant with political possibilities.

The second official unit in the national political hierarchy is the House of Representatives, controlling the purse-strings, which have been the deadly noose of many executive measures. The House is elected every two years, so that it may ever be "near to the people"! This produces a reflex not anticipated by the Fathers of the Constitution. It gives the representative brief respite from the necessities of politics, and hence little time for the necessities of the State.

The House attained the zenith of its power when it arraigned President Johnson at the bar of the Senate for high crimes and misdemeanors in office. It had shackled his appointing power by the Tenure of Office Act; it had forced its plan of reconstruction over his veto; and now it led him, dogged and defiant, to a political trial.

Within a few years the character of the House changed. A new generation interested in the issues of prosperity, rather than those of the war, entered public life. The House grew unwieldy in size and its business increased alarmingly. The minority, meanwhile, retained the power, through filibustering, to hold up the business of the country.

It was under such conditions that Speaker Reed, in 1890, crowned himself "Czar" by compelling a quorum. This he did by counting as actually present all members whom the clerk reported as "present but not voting." The minority fought desperately for its last privilege and even took a case to the Supreme Court to test the constitutionality of a law passed by a Reed-made quorum. The court concurred with the sensible opinion of the country that "when the quorum is present, it is there for the purpose of doing business," an opinion that was completely vindicated when the Democratic minority became a majority and adopted the rule for its own advantage.

By this ruling, the Speakership was lifted to a new eminence. The party caucus, which nominated the Speaker, and to which momentous party questions were referred, gave solidarity to the party. But the influence of the Speaker, through his power of appointing committees, of referring bills, of recognizing members who wished to participate in debate, insured that discipline and centralized authority which makes mass action effective. The power of the Speaker was further enlarged by the creation of the Rules Committee, composed of the Speaker and two members from each party designated by him. This committee formed a triumvirate (the minority members were merely formal members) which set the limits of debate, proposed special rules for such occasions as the committee thought proper, and virtually determined the destiny of bills. So it came about, as Bryce remarks, that the choice of the Speaker was "a political event of the highest significance."

It was under the regency of Speaker Cannon that the power of the Speaker's office attained its climax. The Republicans had a large majority in the House and the old war-horses felt like colts. They assumed their leadership, however, with that obliviousness to youth which usually characterizes old age. The gifted and attractive Reed had ruled often by aphorism and wit, but the unimaginative Cannon ruled by the gavel alone; and in the course of time he and his clique of veterans forgot entirely the difference between power and leadership.

Even party regularity could not long endure such tyranny. It was not against party organization that the insurgents finally raised their lances, but against the arbitrary use of the machinery of the organization by a small group of intrenched "standpatters." The revolt began during the debate on the Payne-Aldrich tariff, and in the campaign of 1908 "Cannonism" was denounced from the stump in every part of the country. By March, 1910, the insurgents were able, with the aid of the Democrats, to amend the rules, increasing the Committee on Rules to ten to be elected by the House and making the Speaker ineligible for membership. When the Democrats secured control of the House in the following year, the rules were revised, and the selection of all committees is now determined by a Committee on Committees chosen in party caucus. This change shifts arbitrary power from the shoulders of the Speaker to the shoulders of the party chieftains. The power of the Speaker has been lessened but by no means destroyed. He is still the party chanticleer.

The political power of the House, however,

cannot be calculated without admitting to the equation the Senate, the third official unit, and, indeed, the most powerful factor in the national hierarchy. The Senate shares equally with the House the responsibility of lawmaking, and shares with the President the responsibility of appointments and of treaty-making. It has been the scene of many memorable contests with the President for political control. The senators are elder statesmen, who have passed through the refining fires of experience, either in law, business, or politics. A senator is elected for six years; so that he has a period of rest between elections, in which he may forget his constituents in the ardor of his duties.

Within the last few decades a great change has come over the Senate, over its membership, its attitude towards public questions, and its relation to the electorate. This has been brought about through disclosures tending to show the relations on the part of some senators towards "big business." As early as the Granger revelations of railway machinations in politics, in the seventies, a popular distrust of the Senate became pronounced. No suggestion of corruption was implied, but certain senators were known as "railway senators," and were believed to use their partizan influence in their friends' behalf. This feeling increased from year to year, until what was long suspected came suddenly to light, through an entirely unexpected agency. William Randolph Hearst, a newspaper owner who had in vain attempted to secure a nomination for President by the Democrats and to get himself elected Governor of New York, had organized and financed a party of his own, the Independence League. While speaking in behalf of his party, in the fall of 1908, he read extracts from letters written by an official of the Standard Oil Company to various senators. The letters, it later appeared, had been purloined from the Company's files by a faithless employee. They caused a tremendous sensation. The public mind had become so sensitive that the mere fact that an intimacy existed between the most notorious of trusts and some few United States senators — the correspondents called each other "Dear John," "Dear Senator," etc. — was sufficient to arouse the general wrath. The letters disclosed a keen interest on the part of the corporation in the details of legislation, and the public promptly took the Standard Oil Company as a type. They believed, without demanding tangible proof, that other great corporations were, in some sinister manner, influencing legislation. Railroads, insurance companies, great banking concerns, vast industrial corporations, were associated in the public mind as "the Interests." And the United States Senate was deemed the stronghold of the interests. A saturnalia of senatorial muckraking now laid bare the "oligarchy," as the small group of powerful veteran Senators who controlled the senatorial machinery was called. It was disclosed that the centralization of leadership in the Senate coincided with the centralization of power in the Democratic and Republican national machines. In 1911 and 1912 a "money trust" investigation was conducted by the Senate and a comfortable *entente* was revealed between a group of bankers, insurance companies, manufacturers, and other interests, carried on through an elaborate system of interlocking directorates. Finally, in 1912, the Senate ordered its Committee on Privileges and Elections to investigate campaign contributions paid to the national campaign committees in 1904, 1908, and 1912. The testimony taken before this committee supplied the country with authentic data of the interrelations of Big Business and Big Politics.

The revolt against "Cannonism" in the House had its counterpart in the Senate. By the time the Aldrich tariff bill came to a vote (1909), about ten Republican senators rebelled. The revolt gathered momentum and culminated in 1912 in the organization of the National Progressive party with Theodore Roosevelt as its candidate for President and Hiram Johnson of California for Vice-President. The majority of the Progressives returned to the Republican fold in 1916. But the rupture was not healed, and the Democrats re-elected Woodrow Wilson.

CHAPTER IX

THE AWAKENING

In the early days a ballot was simply a piece of paper with the names of the candidates written or printed on it. As party organizations became more ambitious, the party printed its own ballots, and "scratching" was done by pasting gummed stickers, with the names of the substitutes printed on them, over the regular ballot, or by simply striking out a name and writing another one in its place. It was customary to print the different party tickets on different colored paper, so that the judges in charge of the ballot boxes could tell how the men voted. When later laws required all ballots to be printed on white paper and of the same size, the parties used paper of different texture. Election officials could then tell by the "feel" which ticket was voted. Finally paper of the same color and quality was enjoined by some States. But it was not until the State itself undertook to print the ballots that uniformity was secured.

In the meantime the peddling of tickets was a regular occupation on election day. Canvassers invaded homes and places of business, and even surrounded the voting place. It was the custom in many parts of the country for the voters to prepare the ballots before reaching the voting-place and carry them in the vest pocket, with a margin showing. This was a sort of signal that the voter's mind had been made up and that he should be let alone, yet even with this signal showing, in hotly contested elections the voter ran a noisy gauntlet of eager solicitors, harassing him on his way to vote as cab drivers assail the traveler when he alights from the train. This free and easy method, tolerable in sparsely settled pioneer districts, failed miserably in the cities. It was necessary to pass rigorous laws against vote buying and selling, and to clear the polling-place of all partizan soliciting. Penal provisions were enacted against intimidation, violence, repeating, false swearing when challenged, ballot-box stuffing, and the more patent forms of partizan vices. In order to stop the practice of "repeating," New York early passed laws requiring voters to be duly registered.

But the early laws were defective, and the rolls were easily padded. In most of the cities poll lists were made by the party workers, and the name of each voter was checked off as he voted. It was still impossible for the voter to keep secret his ballot. The buyer of votes could tell whether he got what he paid for; the employer, so disposed, could bully those dependent on him into voting as he wished, and the way was open to all manner of tricks in the printing of ballots with misleading emblems, or with certain names omitted, or with a mixture of candidates from various parties — tricks that were later forbidden by law but were none the less common.

Rather suddenly a great change came over election day. In 1888 Kentucky adopted the Australian ballot for the city of Louisville, and Massachusetts adopted it for all state and local elections. The Massachusetts statute provided that before an election each political party should certify its nominees to the Secretary of the Commonwealth. The State then printed the ballots. All the nominees of all the parties were printed on one sheet. Each office was placed in a separate column, the candidates in alphabetical order, with the names of the parties following. Blank spaces were left for those who wished to vote for others than the regular nominees. This form of ballot prevented "voting straight" with a single mark. The voter, in the seclusion of a booth at the polling-place, had to pick his party's candidates from the numerous columns.

Indiana, in 1889, adopted a similar statute but the ballot had certain modifications to suit the needs of party orthodoxy. Here the columns represented parties, not offices. Each party had a column. Each column was headed by the party name and its device, so that those who could not read could vote for the Rooster or the Eagle or the Fountain. There was a circle placed under the device, and by making his mark in this circle the voter voted straight.

Within eight years thirty-eight States and two Territories had adopted the Australian or blanket ballot in some modified form. It was but a step to the state control of the election machinery. Some state officer, usually the Secretary of State, was designated to see that the election laws were enforced. In New York a State Commissioner of Elections was appointed. The appointment of local inspectors and judges remained for a time in the hands of the parties. But soon in several

States even this power was taken from them, and the trend now is towards appointing all election officers by the central authority. These officers also have complete charge of the registration of voters. In some States, like New York, registration has become a rather solemn procedure, requiring the answering of many questions and the signing of the voter's name, all under the threat of perjury if a wilful misrepresentation is made.

So passed out of the control of the party the preparation of the ballot and the use of the ballot on election day. Innumerable rules have been laid down by the State for the conduct of elections. The distribution of the ballots, their custody before election, the order of electional procedure, the counting of the ballots, the making of returns, the custody of the ballot-boxes, and all other necessary details, are regulated by law under official state supervision. The parties are allowed watchers at the polls, but these have no official standing.

If a Revolutionary Father could visit his old haunts on election day, he would be astonished at the sober decorum. In his time elections lasted three days, days filled with harangue, with drinking, betting, raillery, and occasional encounters.

Even those whose memory goes back to the Civil War can contrast the ballot peddling, the soliciting, the crowded noisy polling-places, with the calm and quiet with which men deposit their ballots today. For now every ballot is numbered and no one is permitted to take a single copy from the room. Every voter must prepare his ballot in the booth. And every polling-place is an island of immunity in the sea of political excitement.

While the people were thus assuming control of the ballot, they were proceeding to gain control of their legislatures. In 1890 Massachusetts enacted one of the first antilobby laws. It has served as a model for many other States. It provided that the sergeant-at-arms should keep dockets in which were enrolled the names of all persons employed as counsel or agents before legislative committees. Each counsel or agent was further compelled to state the length of his engagement, the subjects or bills for which he was employed, and the name and address of his employer.

The first session after the passage of this law, many of the professional lobbyists refused to enroll, and the most notorious ones were seen no more in the State House. The regular counsel of railroads, insurance companies, and other interests signed the proper docket and appeared for their clients in open committee meetings.

The law made it the duty of the Secretary of the Commonwealth to report to the law officers of the State, for prosecution, all those who failed to comply with the act. Sixty-seven such delinquents were reported the first year. The Grand Jury refused to indict them, but the number of recalcitrants has gradually diminished.

The experience of Massachusetts is not unique. Other States passed more or less rigorous anti-lobby laws, and today, in no state Capitol, will the visitor see the disgusting sights that were usual thirty years ago — arrogant and coarse professional "agents" mingling on the floor of the legislature with members, even suggesting procedure to presiding officers, and not infrequently commandeering a majority. Such influences, where they persist, have been driven under cover.

With the decline of the professional lobbyist came the rise of the volunteer lobbyist. Important bills are now considered in formal committee hearings which are well advertised so that interested parties may be present. Publicity and information have taken the place of secrecy in legislative procedure. The gathering of expert testimony by special legislative commissions of inquiry is now a frequent practice in respect to subjects of wide social import, such as workmen's compensation, widows' pensions, and factory conditions.

A number of States have resorted to the initiative and referendum as applied to ordinary legislation. By means of this method a small percentage of the voters, from eight to ten per cent, may initiate proposals and impose upon the voters the function of legislation. South Dakota, in 1898, made constitutional provision for direct legislation. Utah followed in 1900, Oregon in 1902, Nevada in 1904, Montana in 1906, and Oklahoma in 1907. East of the Mississippi, several States have adopted a modified form of the initiative and referendum. In Oregon, where this device of direct government has been most assiduously applied, the voters in 1908 voted upon nineteen different bills and constitutional amendments; in 1910 the number increased to thirty-two; in 1912, to thirty-seven; in 1914 it fell to twenty-nine. The vote cast for these measures rarely exceeded eighty per cent of those voting at the election and frequently fell below sixty.

The electorate that attempts to rid itself of the evils of the state legislature by these heroic

methods assumes a heavy responsibility. When
the burden of direct legislation is added to the task
of choosing from the long list of elective officers
which is placed before the voter at every local
and state election, it is not surprising that there
should set in a reaction in favor of simplified government. The mere separation of state and local
elections does not solve the problem. It somewhat
minimizes the chances of partizan influence over
the voter in local elections; but the voter is still
confronted with the long lists of candidates for
elective offices. Ballots not infrequently contain two hundred names, sometimes even three
hundred or more, covering candidates of four or
five parties for scores of offices. These blanket
ballots are sometimes three feet long. After an
election in Chicago in 1916, one of the leading
dailies expressed sympathy "for the voter emerg-
ing from the polling-booth, clutching a handful of
papers, one of them about half as large as a bed
sheet." Probably most voters were able to express
a real preference among the national candidates.
It is almost equally certain that most voters
were not able to express a real preference among
important local administrative officials. A huge
ballot, all printed over with names, supplemented

by a series of smaller ballots, can never be a manageable instrument even for an electorate as intelligent as ours.

Simplification is the prophetic watchword in state government today. For cities, the City Manager and the Commission have offered salvation. A few officers only are elected and these are held strictly responsible, sometimes under the constant threat of the recall, for the entire administration. Over four hundred cities have adopted the form of government by Commission. But nothing has been done to simplify our state governments, which are surrounded by a maze of heterogeneous and undirected boards and authorities. Every time the legislature found itself confronted by a new function to be cared for, it simply created a new board. New York has a hodgepodge of over 116 such authorities; Minnesota, 75; Illinois, 100. Iowa in 1913 and Illinois and Minnesota in 1914, indeed, perfected elaborate proposals for simplifying their state governments. But these suggestions remain dormant. And the New York State Constitutional Convention in 1915 prepared a new Constitution for the State, with the same end in view, but their work was not accepted by the people. It may be said, however, that in our attempt to rid ourselves of boss rule we have swung through the arc of direct government and are now on the returning curve toward representative government, a more intensified representative government that makes evasion of responsibility and duty impossible by fixing it upon one or two men.

CHAPTER X

PARTY REFORM

THE State, at first, had paid little attention to the party, which was regarded as a purely voluntary aggregation of like-minded citizens. Evidently the State could not dictate that you should be a Democrat or a Republican or force you to be an Independent. With the adoption of the Australian ballot, however, came the legal recognition of the party; for as soon as the State recognized the party's designated nominees in the preparation of the official ballot, it recognized the party. It was then discovered that, unless some restrictions were imposed, groups of interested persons in the old parties would manage the nominations of both to their mutual satisfaction. Thus a handful of Democrats would visit Republican caucuses or primaries and a handful of Republicans would return the favor to the Democrats. In other words, the bosses of both parties would coöperate in order to secure nominations satisfactory to themselves.

Massachusetts began the reform by defining a party as a group of persons who had cast a certain percentage of the votes at the preceding election. This definition has been widely accepted; and the number of votes has been variously fixed at from two to twenty-five per cent. Other States have followed the New York plan of fixing definitely the number of voters necessary to form a party. In New York no fewer than 10,000 voters can secure recognition as a state party, exception being made in favor of municipal or purely local parties. But merely fixing the numerical minimum of the party was not enough. The State took another step forward in depriving the manipulator of his liberty when it undertook to determine who was entitled to membership in the party and privileged to take part in its nominations and other party procedure. Otherwise the virile minority in each party would control both the membership and the nominations.

An Oregon statute declares: "Every political party and every volunteer political organization has the same right to be protected from the interference of persons who are not identified with it, as its known and publicly avowed members, that the government of the State has to protect itself from the interference of persons who are not known and registered as its electors. It is as great a wrong to the people, as well as to members of a political party, for anyone who is not known to be one of its members to vote or take any part at any election, or other proceedings of such political party, as it is for one who is not a qualified and registered elector to vote at any state election or to take part in the business of the State." It is a far reach from the democratic *laissez faire* of Jackson's day to this state dogmatism which threatens the independent or detached voter with ultimate extinction.

A variety of methods have been adopted for initiating the citizen into party membership. In the Southern States, where the dual party system does not exist, the legislature has left the matter in the hands of the duly appointed party officials. They can, with canonical rigor, determine the party standing of voters at the primaries. But where there is party competition, such a generous endowment of power would be dangerous.

Many States permit the voter to make his declaration of party allegiance when he goes to the primary. He asks for the ticket of the party whose nominees he wishes to help select. He is then handed the party's ballot, which he marks and places in the ballot-box of that party. Now, if he is challenged, he must declare upon oath that he is a member of that party, that he has generally supported its tickets and its principles, and that at the coming election he intends to support at least a majority of its nominees. In this method little freedom is left to the voter who wishes to participate as an independent both in the primaries and in the general election.

The New York plan is more rigorous. Here, in all cities, the voter enrolls his name on his party's lists when he goes to register for the coming election. He receives a ballot upon which are the following words: "I am in general sympathy with the principles of the party which I have designated by my mark hereunder; it is my intention to support generally at the next general election, state and national, the nominees of such party for state and national offices; and I have not enrolled with or participated in any primary election or convention of any other party since the first day of last year." On this enrollment blank he indicates the party of his choice, and the election officials deposit all the ballots, after sealing them in envelopes, in a special box. At a time designated by law, these seals are broken and the party enrollment is compiled from them. These party enrollment books are public records. Everyone who cares may consult the lists. The advantages of secrecy — such as they are — are thus not secured.

It remained for Wisconsin, the experimenting State, to find a way of insuring secrecy. Here, when the voter goes to the primary, he is handed a large ballot, upon which all the party nominations are printed. The different party tickets are separated by perforations, so that the voter simply tears out the party ticket he wishes to vote, marks it, and puts it in the box. The rejected tickets he deposits in a large waste basket provided for the discards.

While the party was being fenced in by legal definition, its machinery, the intricate hierarchy of committees, was subjected to state scrutiny with the avowed object of ridding the party of ring rule. The State Central Committee is the key to the situation. To democratize this committee is a task that has severely tested the ingenuity of the State, for the inventive capacity of the professional politician is prodigious. The devices to circumvent the politician are so numerous and various that only a few types can be selected to illustrate how the State is carrying out its determination.   Illinois has provided perhaps the most democratic method.   In each congressional district, the voters, at the regular party primaries, choose the member of the state committee for the district, who serves for a term of two years.   The law says that "no other person or persons whomsoever" than those so chosen by the voters shall serve on the committee, so that members by courtesy or by proxy, who might represent the boss, are apparently shut off.   The law stipulates the time within which the committee must meet and organize.   Under this plan, if the ring controls the committee, the fault lies wholly with the majority of the party; it is a self-imposed thraldom.

Iowa likewise stipulates that the Central Committee shall be composed of one member from each congressional district.   But the members are chosen in a state convention, organized under strict and minute regulations imposed by law.   It permits considerable freedom to the committee, however, stating that it "may organize at pleasure for political work as is usual and customary with such committees."

In Wisconsin another plan was adopted in 1907. Here the candidates for the various state offices and for both branches of the legislature and the senators whose terms have not expired meet in the state capital at noon on a day specified by law and elect by ballot a central committee consisting of at least two members from each congressional district. A chairman is chosen in the same manner.

Most States, however, leave some leeway in the choice of the state committee, permitting their election usually by the regular primaries but controlling their action in many details. The lesser committees — county, city, district, judicial, senatorial, congressional, and others — are even more rigorously controlled by law.

So the issuing of the party platform, the principles on which it must stand or fall, has been touched by this process of ossification. Few States retain the state convention in its original vigor. In all States where primaries are held for state nominations, the emasculated and subdued convention is permitted to write the party platform. But not so in some States. Wisconsin permits the candidates and the hold-over members of the Senate, assembled according to law in a state meeting, to

issue the platform.   In other States, the Central
Committee and the various candidates for state
office form a party council and frame the platform.
Oregon, in 1901, tried a novel method of providing
platforms by referendum.   But the courts declared
the law unconstitutional.   So Oregon now permits
each candidate to write his own platform in not
over one hundred words and file it with his nominating petition, and to present a statement
of not over twelve words to be printed on the
ballot.

The convention system provided many opportunities for the manipulator and was inherently
imperfect for nominating more than one or two candidates for office.   It has survived as the method
of nominating candidates for President of the
United States because it is adapted to the wide
geographical range of the nation and because in the
national convention only a President and a Vice-
President are nominated.   In state and county conventions, where often candidates for a dozen or
more offices are to be nominated, it was often
subject to demoralizing bartering.

The larger the number of nominations to be
made, the more complete was the jobbery, and
this was the death-warrant of the local convention.

These evils were recognized as early as June 20, 1860, when the Republican county convention of Crawford County, Pennsylvania, adopted the following resolutions:

Whereas, in nominating candidates for the several county offices, it clearly is, or ought to be, the object to arrive as nearly as possible at the wishes of the majority, or at least a plurality of the Republican voters; and

Whereas the present system of nominating by delegates, who virtually represent territory rather than votes, and who almost necessarily are wholly unacquainted with the wishes and feelings of their constituents in regard to various candidates for office, is undemocratic, because the people have no voice in it, and objectionable, because men are often placed in nomination because of their location who are decidedly unpopular, even in their own districts, and because it affords too great an opportunity for scheming and designing men to accomplish their own purposes; therefore

Resolved, that we are in favor of submitting nominations directly to the people — the Republican voters — and that delegate conventions for nominating county officers be abolished, and we hereby request and instruct the county committee to issue their call in 1861, in accordance with the spirit of this resolution.

Upon the basis of this indictment of the county convention system, the Republican voters of Crawford County, a rural community, whose largest town is Meadville, the county seat, proceeded to nominate their candidates by direct vote, under rules prepared by the county committee. These rules have been but slightly changed. The informality of a hat or open table drawer has been replaced by an official ballot-box, and an official ballot has taken the place of the tickets furnished by each candidate.

The "Crawford County plan," as it was generally called, was adopted by various localities in many States. In 1866 California and New York enacted laws to protect primaries and nominating caucuses from fraud. In 1871 Ohio and Pennsylvania enacted similar laws, followed by Missouri in 1875 and New Jersey in 1878. By 1890 over a dozen States had passed laws attempting to eliminate the grosser frauds attendant upon making nominations. In many instances it was made optional with the party whether the direct plan should supersede the delegate plan. Only in certain cities, however, was the primary made mandatory in these States. By far the larger areas retained the convention.

There is noticeable in these years a gradual increase in the amount of legislation concerning the nominating machinery — prescribing the days and hours for holding elections of delegates, the size of the polling-place, the nature of the ballot-box, the poll-list, who might participate in the choice of delegates, how the returns were to be made, and so on. By the time, then, that the Australian ballot came, with its profound changes, nearly all the States had attempted to remove the glaring abuses of the nominating system; and several of them officially recognized the direct primary. The State was reluctant to abolish the convention system entirely; and the Crawford County plan long remained merely optional. But in 1901 Minnesota enacted a state-wide, mandatory primary law. Mississippi followed in 1902, Wisconsin in 1903, and Oregon in 1904. This movement has swept the country.

Few States retain the nominating convention, and where it remains it is shackled by legal restrictions. The boss, however, has devised adequate means for controlling primaries, and a return to a modified convention system is being earnestly discussed in many States to circumvent the further ingenuity of the boss.

A further step towards the state control of parties was taken when laws began to busy themselves with the conduct of the campaign. Corrupt Practices Acts began to assume bulk in the early nineties, to limit the expenditure of candidates, and to enumerate the objects for which campaign committees might legitimately spend money. These are usually personal traveling expenses of the candidates, rental of rooms for committees and halls for meetings, payment of musicians and speakers and their traveling expenses, printing campaign material, postage for distribution of letters, newspapers and printed matter, telephone and telegraph charges, political advertising, employing challengers at the polls, necessary clerk hire, and conveyances for bringing aged or infirm voters to the polls. The maximum amount that can be spent by candidates is fixed, and they are required to make under oath a detailed statement of their expenses in both primary and general elections. The various committees, also, must make detailed reports of the funds they handle, the amount, the contributors, and the expenditures. Corporations are forbidden to contribute, and the amount that candidates themselves may give is limited in many States. These exactions are reinforced by strin-

gent laws against bribery. Persons found guilty
of either receiving or soliciting a bribe are generally
disfranchised or declared ineligible for public office
for a term of years. Illinois, for the second offense,
forever disfranchises.

It is not surprising that these restrictions have
led the State to face the question whether it should
not itself bear some of the expenses of the campaign. It has, of course, already assumed an
enormous burden formerly borne entirely by the
party. The cost of primary and general elections
nowadays is tremendous. A few Western States
print a campaign pamphlet and distribute it to
every voter. The pamphlet contains usually the
photographs of the candidates, a brief biography,
and a statement of principles.

These are the principal encroachments made by
the Government upon the autonomy of the party.
The details are endless. The election laws of New
York fill 330 printed pages. It is little wonder
that American parties are beginning to study the
organization of European parties, such as the labor
parties and the social democratic parties, which
have enlisted a rather fervent party fealty. These
are propagandist parties and require to be active
all the year round. So they demand annual dues

of their members and have permanent salaried officials and official party organs. Such a permanent organization was suggested for the National Progressive party. But the early disintegration of the party made impossible what would have been an interesting experiment. After the election of 1916, Governor Whitman of New York suggested that the Republican party choose a manager and pay him $10,000 a year and have a lien on all his time and energy. The plan was widely discussed and its severest critics were the politicians who would suffer from it. The wide-spread comment with which it was received revealed the change that has come over the popular idea of a political party since the State began forty years ago to bring the party under its control.

But flexibility is absolutely essential to a party system that adequately serves a growing democracy. And under a two-party system, as ours is probably bound to remain, the independent voter usually holds the balance of power. He may be merely a disgruntled voter seeking for revenge, or an overpleased voter seeking to maintain a profitable *status quo*, or he may belong to that class of super-citizens from which mugwumps arise. In any case, the majorities at elections are usually determined by him. And party orthodoxy made by the State is almost as distasteful to him as the rigor of the boss. He relishes neither the one nor the other.

In the larger cities the citizens' tickets and fusion movements are types of independent activities. In some cities they are merely temporary associations, formed for a single, thorough house-cleaning. The Philadelphia Committee of One Hundred, which was organized in 1880 to fight the Gas Ring, is an example. It issued a Declaration of Principles, demanding the promotion of public service rather than private greed, and the prosecution of "those who have been guilty of election frauds, maladministration of office, or misappropriation of public funds." Announcing that it would endorse only candidates who signed this declaration, the committee supported the Democratic candidates, and nominated for Receiver of Taxes a candidate of its own, who became also the Democratic nominee when the regular Democratic candidate withdrew. Philadelphia was overwhelmingly Republican. But the committee's aid was powerful enough to elect the Democratic candidate for mayor by 6000 majority and the independent candidate for Receiver of Taxes by 20,000.

This gave the Committee access to the records of the doings of the Gas Ring. In 1884, however, the candidate which it endorsed was defeated, and it disbanded.

Similar in experience was the famous New York Committee of Seventy, organized in 1894 after Dr. Parkhurst's lurid disclosures of police connivance with every degrading vice. A call was issued by thirty-three well-known citizens for a non-partizan mass meeting, and at this meeting a committee of seventy was appointed "with full power to confer with other anti-Tammany organizations, and to take such actions as may be necessary to further the objects of this meeting as set forth in the call therefor, and the address adopted by this meeting." The committee adopted a platform, appointed an executive and a finance committee, and nominated a full ticket, distributing the candidates among both parties. All other anti-Tammany organizations endorsed this ticket, and it was elected by large majorities. The committee dissolved after having secured certain charter amendments for the city and seeing its roster of officers inaugurated.

The Municipal Voters' League of Chicago is an important example of the permanent type of citizens' organization. The league is composed of voters in every ward, who, acting through committees and alert officers, scrutinize every candidate for city office from the Mayor down. It does not aim to nominate a ticket of its own, but to exercise such vigilance, enforced by so effective an organization and such wide-reaching publicity, that the various parties will, of their own volition, nominate men whom the league can endorse. By thus putting on the hydraulic pressure of organized public opinion, it has had a considerable influence on the parties and a very stimulating effect on the citizenry.

Finally, there has developed in recent years the fusion movement, whereby the opponents of boss rule in all parties unite and back an independent or municipal ticket. The election of Mayor Mitchel of New York in 1913 was thus accomplished. In Milwaukee, a fusion has been successful against the Socialists. And in many lesser cities this has brought at least temporary relief from the oppression of the local oligarchy.

12

CHAPTER XI

THE EXPERT AT LAST

THE administrative weakness of a democracy, namely, the tendency towards a government by job-hunters, was disclosed even in the early days of the United States, when the official machinery was simple and the number of offices few. Washington at once foresaw both the difficulties and the duties that the appointing power imposed. Soon after his inauguration he wrote to Rutledge: "I anticipate that one of the most difficult and delicate parts of the duty of any office will be that which relates to nominations for appointments." And he was most scrupulous and painstaking in his appointments. Fitness for duty was paramount with him, though he recognized geographical necessity and distributed the offices with that precision which characterized all his acts.

John Adams made very few appointments. After his term had expired, he wrote: "Washington appointed a multitude of Democrats and Jacobins of the deepest die. I have been more cautious in this respect."

The test of partizan loyalty, however, was not applied generally until after the election of Jefferson. The ludicrous apprehensions of the Federalists as to what would follow upon his election were not allayed by his declared intentions. "I have given," he wrote to Monroe, "and will give only to Republicans under existing circumstances." Jefferson was too good a politician to overlook his opportunity to annihilate the Federalists. He hoped to absorb them in his own party, "to unite the names of Federalists and Republicans." Moderate Federalists, who possessed sufficient gifts of grace for conversion, he sedulously nursed. But he removed all officers for whose removal any special reason could be discovered. The "midnight appointments" of John Adams he refused to acknowledge, and he paid no heed to John Marshall's dicta in Marbury *versus* Madison. He was zealous in discovering plausible excuses for making vacancies. The New York *Evening Post* described him as "gazing round, with wild anxiety furiously inquiring, 'how are vacancies to be obtained?'"

Directly and indirectly, Jefferson effected, during his first term, 164 changes in the offices at his disposal, a large number for those days. This he did so craftily, with such delicate regard for geographical sensitiveness and with such a nice balance between fitness for office and the desire for office, that by the end of his second term he had not only consolidated our first disciplined and eager political party, but had quieted the storm against his policy of partizan proscription.

During the long régime of the Jeffersonian Republicans there were three significant movements. In January, 1811, Nathaniel Macon introduced his amendment to the Constitution providing that no member of Congress should receive a civil appointment "under the authority of the United States until the expiration of the presidential term in which such person shall have served as senator or representative." An amendment was offered by Josiah Quincy, making ineligible to appointment the relations by blood or marriage of any senator or representative. Nepotism was considered the curse of the civil service, and for twenty years similar amendments were discussed at almost every session of Congress. John Quincy Adams said that half of the members wanted office, and the other half wanted office for their relatives.

In 1820 the Four Years' Act substituted a four-year tenure of office, in place of a term at the pleasure of the President, for most of the federal appointments. The principal argument urged in favor of the law was that unsatisfactory civil servants could easily be dropped without reflection on their character. Defalcations had been discovered to the amount of nearly a million dollars, due mainly to carelessness and gross inefficiency. It was further argued that any efficient incumbent need not be disquieted, for he would be reappointed. The law, however, fulfilled Jefferson's prophecy: it kept "in constant excitement all the hungry cormorants for office."

What Jefferson began, Jackson consummated. The stage was now set for Democracy. Public office had been marshaled as a force in party maneuver. In his first annual message, Jackson announced his philosophy:

There are perhaps few men who can for any great length of time enjoy office and power without being more or less under the influence of feelings unfavorable to the faithful discharge of their public duties. . . . Office is considered as a species of property, and government rather as a means of promoting individual interests than as an instrument created solely for the service of the people. Corruption in some, and in others a perversion of correct feelings and principles, divert government from its legitimate ends and make it an engine for the support of the few at the expense of the many. The duties of all public offices are, or at least admit of being made, so plain, so simple that men of intelligence may readily qualify themselves for their performance. . . . In a country where offices are created solely for the benefit of the people, no one man has any more intrinsic right to official station than another.

The Senate refused Jackson's request for an extension of the Four Years' law to cover all positions in the civil service. It also refused to confirm some of his appointments, notably that of Van Buren as minister to Great Britain. The debate upon this appointment gave the spoilsman an epigram. Clay with directness pointed to Van Buren as the introducer "of the odious system of proscription for the exercise of the elective franchise in the government of the United States." He continued: "I understand it is the system on which the party in his own State, of which he is the reputed head, constantly acts. He was among the first of the secretaries to apply that system to the dismission of clerks of his department . . .

known to me to be highly meritorious . . . It is a detestable system."

And Webster thundered: "I pronounce my rebuke as solemnly and as decisively as I can upon this first instance in which an American minister has been sent abroad as the representative of his party and not as the representative of his country."

To these and other challenges, Senator Marcy of New York made his well-remembered retort that "the politicians of the United States are not so fastidious. . . . They see nothing wrong in the rule that to the victor belong the spoils of the enemy."

Jackson, with all his bluster and the noise of his followers, made his proscriptions relatively fewer than those of Jefferson. He removed only 252 of about 612 presidential appointees.[1] It should, however, be remembered that those who were not removed had assured Jackson's agents of their loyalty to the new Democracy.

If Jackson did not inaugurate the spoils system, he at least gave it a mission. It was to save the country from the curse of officialdom. His suc-

[1] This does not include deputy postmasters, who numbered about 8000 and were not placed in the presidential list until 1836.

cessor, Van Buren, brought the system to a perfection that only the experienced politician could
achieve. Van Buren required of all appointees
partizan service; and his own nomination, at
Baltimore, was made a foregone conclusion by the
host of federal job-holders who were delegates.
Van Buren simply introduced at Washington the
methods of the Albany Regency.

The Whigs blustered bravely against this
proscription. But their own President, General
Harrison, "Old Tippecanoe," was helpless against
the saturnalia of office-seekers that engulfed him.
Harrison, when he came to power, removed about
one-half of the officials in the service. And, although the partizan color of the President changed
with Harrison's death, after a few weeks in office,
— Tyler was merely a Whig of convenience — there
was no change in the President's attitude towards
the spoils system.

Presidential inaugurations became orgies of
office-seekers, and the first weeks of every new
term were given over to distributing the jobs,
ordinary business having to wait. President Polk,
who removed the usual quota, is complimented by
Webster for making "rather good selections from
his own friends." The practice, now firmly es-

tablished, was continued by Taylor, Pierce, and Buchanan.

Lincoln found himself surrounded by circumstances that made caution necessary in every appointment. His party was new and composed of many diverse elements. He had to transform their jealousies into enthusiasm, for the approach of civil war demanded supreme loyalty and unity of action. To this greater cause of saving the Union he bent every effort and used every instrumentality at his command. No one before him had made so complete a change in the official personnel of the capital as the change which he was constrained to make. No one before him or since used the appointing power with such consummate skill or displayed such rare tact and knowledge of human nature in seeking the advice of those who deemed their advice valuable. The war greatly increased the number of appointments, and it also imposed obligations that made merit sometimes a secondary consideration. With the statesman's vision, Lincoln recognized both the use and the abuse of the patronage system. He declined to gratify the office-seekers who thronged the capital at the beginning of his second term; and they returned home disappointed.

The twenty years following the Civil War were years of agitation for reform. People were at last recognizing the folly of using the multiplying public offices for party spoils. The quarrel between Congress and President Johnson over removals, and the Tenure of Office Act, focused popular attention on the constitutional question of appointment and removal, and the recklessness of the political manager during Grant's two terms disgusted the thoughtful citizen.

The first attempts to apply efficiency to the civil service had been made when pass examinations were used for sifting candidates for clerkships in the Treasury Department in 1853, when such tests were prescribed by law for the lowest grade of clerkships. The head of the department was given complete control over the examinations, and they were not exacting. In 1864 Senator Sumner introduced a bill "to provide for the greater efficiency of the civil service." It was considered chimerical and dropped.

Meanwhile, a steadfast and able champion of reform appeared in the House, Thomas A. Jenckes, a prominent lawyer of Rhode Island. A bill which he introduced in December, 1865, received no hearing. But in the following year a select

joint committee was charged to examine the whole
question of appointments, dismissals, and patronage. Mr. Jenckes presented an elaborate report
in May, 1868, explaining the civil service of other
countries. This report, which is the corner stone
of American civil service reform, provided the
material for congressional debate and threw the
whole subject into the public arena. Jenckes in
the House and Carl Schurz in the Senate saw to
it that ardent and convincing defense of reform
was not wanting. In compliance with President
Grant's request for a law to "govern not the
tenure, but the manner of making all appointments," a rider was attached to the appropriation
bill in 1870, asking the President "to prescribe
such rules and regulations" as he saw fit, and "to
employ suitable persons to conduct" inquiries
into the best method for admitting persons into
the civil service. A commission of which George
William Curtis was chairman made recommendations, but they were not adopted and Curtis
resigned. The New York Civil Service Reform
Association was organized in 1877; and the National League, organized in 1881, soon had flourish-
ing branches in most of the large cities. The battle
was largely between the President and Congress.

Each succeeding President signified his adherence to reform, but neutralized his words by sanctioning vast changes in the service. Finally, under circumstances already described, on January 16, 1883, the Civil Service Act was passed.

This law had a stimulating effect upon state and municipal civil service. New York passed a law the same year, patterned after the federal act. Massachusetts followed in 1884, and within a few years many of the States had adopted some sort of civil service reform, and the large cities were experimenting with the merit system. It was not, however, until the rapid expansion of the functions of government and the consequent transformation in the nature of public duties that civil service reform made notable headway. When the Government assumed the duties of health officer, forester, statistician, and numerous other highly specialized functions, the presence of the scientific expert became imperative; and vast undertakings, like the building of the Panama Canal and the enormous irrigation projects of the West, could not be entrusted to the spoilsman and his minions.

The war has accustomed us to the commandeering of utilities, of science, and of skill upon a colossal scale. From this height of public devotion it is

mprobable that we shall decline, after the national
peril has passed, into the depths of administrative
ncompetency which our Republic, and all its
parts, occupied for so many years. The need for
an efficient and highly complex State has been
driven home to the consciousness of the average
citizen. And this foretokens the permanent enlist-
ment of talent in the public service to the end that
democracy may provide that effective nationalism
imposed by the new era of world competition.

BIBLIOGRAPHICAL NOTE

THERE is no collected material of the literature of exposure. It is found in the official reports of investigating committees, such as the Lexow, Mazet, and Fassett committees in New York, and the report on campaign contributions by the Senate Committee on Privileges and Elections (1913). The muckraker has scattered such indiscriminate charges that great caution is necessary to discover the truth. Only testimony taken under oath can be relied upon. And for local exposés the official court records must be sought.

The annual proceedings of the National Municipal League contain a great deal of useful material on municipal politics. The reports of local organizations, such as the New York Bureau of Municipal Research and the Pittsburgh Voters' League, are invaluable, as are the reports of occasional bodies, like the Philadelphia Committee of Fifty.

Personal touches can be gleaned from the autobiographies of such public men as Platt, Foraker, Weed, La Follette, and in such biographies as Croly's *M. A. Hanna*.

On Municipal Conditions:

W. B. MUNRO, *The Government of American Cities* (1913). An authoritative and concise account of the development of American city government. Chapter VII deals with municipal politics.

J. J. HAMILTON, *Dethronement of the City Boss* (1910). A description of the operation of commission government.

E. S. BRADFORD, *Commission Government in American Cities* (1911). A careful study of the commission plan.

H. BRUÈRE, *New City Government* (1912). An interesting account of the new municipal régime.

LINCOLN STEFFENS, *The Shame of the Cities* and *The Struggle for Self-Government* (1906). The Prince of the Muckrakers' contribution to the literature of awakening.

On State Conditions:

There is an oppressive barrenness of material on this subject.

P. S. REINSCH, *American Legislatures and Legislativ Methods* (1907). A brilliant exposition of the legislatures' activities.

E. L. GODKIN, *Unforeseen Tendencies in Democrac* contains a thoughtful essay on "The Decline of Legislatures."

On Political Parties and Machines:

M. OSTROGORSKI, *Democracy and the Organization of Political Parties*, 2 vols. (1902). The second volum contains a comprehensive and able survey of the American party system. It has been abridged into single volume edition called *Democracy and the Part System in the United States* (1910).

JAMES BRYCE, *The American Commonwealth*, 2 vol

Volume II contains a noteworthy account of our political system.

JESSE MACY, *Party Organization and Machinery* (1912). A succinct account of party machinery.

J. A. WOODBURN, *Political Parties and Party Problems* (1906). A sane account of our political task.

P. O. RAY, *An Introduction to Political Parties and Practical Politics* (1913). Valuable for its copious references to current literature on political subjects.

THEODORE ROOSEVELT, *Essays on Practical Politics* (1888). Vigorous description of machine methods.

G. M. GREGORY, *The Corrupt Use of Money in Politics and Laws for its Prevention* (1893). Written before the later exposés, it nevertheless gives a clear view of the problem.

W. M. IVINS, *Machine Politics* (1897). In New York City — by a keen observer.

GEORGE VICKERS, *The Fall of Bossism* (1883). On the overthrow of the Philadelphia Gas Ring.

GUSTAVUS MYERS, *History of Tammany Hall* (1901; revised 1917). The best book on the subject.

E. C. GRIFFITH, *The Rise and Development of the Gerrymander* (1907).

Historical:

H. J. FORD, *Rise and Growth of American Politics* (1898). One of the earliest and one of the best accounts of the development of American politics.

ALEXANDER JOHNSTON and J. A. WOODBURN, *American Political History*, 2 vols. (1905). A brilliant recital of American party history. The most satisfactory book on the subject.

13

W. M. Sloane, *Party Government in the United States* (1914). A concise and convenient recital. Brings our party history to date.

J. B. McMaster, *With the Fathers* (1896). A volume of delightful historical essays, including one on "The Political Depravity of the Fathers."

On Nominations:

F. W. Dallinger, *Nominations for Elective Office in the United States* (1897). The most thorough work on the subject, describing the development of our nominating systems.

C. E. Merriam, *Primary Elections* (1908). A concise description of the primary and its history.

R. S. Childs, *Short Ballot Principles* (1911). A splendid account by the father of the short ballot movement.

C. E. Meyer, *Nominating Systems* (1902). Good on the caucus.

On the Presidency:

J. B. Bishop, *Our Political Drama* (1904). A readable account of national conventions and presidential campaigns.

A. K. McClure, *Our Presidents and How We Make Them* (1903).

Edward Stanwood, *A History of the Presidency* (1898). Gives party platforms and describes each presidential campaign.

On Congress:

G. H. Haynes, *The Election of United States Senators* (1906).

H. J. FORD, *The Cost of Our National Government*
(1910). A fine account of congressional bad housekeeping.

MARY C. FOLLETT, *The Speaker of the House of Representatives* (1896).

WOODROW WILSON, *Congressional Government* (1885).
Most interesting reading in the light of the Wilson
Administration.

L. G. MCCONACHIE, *Congressional Committees* (1898).

On Special Topics:

C. R. FISH, *Civil Service and the Patronage* (1905).
The best work on the subject.

J. D. BARNETT, *The Operation of the Initiative, Referendum, and Recall in Oregon* (1915). A helpful, intensive
study of these important questions.

E. P. OBERHOLTZER, *The Referendum in America*
(1912). The most satisfactory and comprehensive
work on the subject. Also discusses the initiative.

J. R. COMMONS, *Proportional Representation* (1907).
The standard American book on the subject.

R. C. BROOKS, *Corruption in American Politics and
Life* (1910). A survey of our political pathology.

INDEX

Abolitionists, in Republican party, 13

Adams, John, Federalist candidate, 21–22; contest over election, 134; appointments by, 178–79.

Adams, J. Q., elected President, 9

Adams, Samuel, 120

Albany Argus, 31

Albany Journal, 123

"Albany Regency," 30–31, 184

American party, 13, 17

Ames, "Doc," Boss of Minneapolis, 111–14

Ames, Oakes, of Mass., 42–44

"Andrews Jury," 108

Anti-Federalist party, in Constitutional Convention, 4; types composing, 4; becomes Democratic-Republican party, 6

Anti-Masonic party, 16–17, 23

"April Grand Jury," 113–14

Armstrong Committee, 124

Articles of Confederation, 3

Ashbridge, "Stars-and-Stripes Sam," Mayor of Philadelphia, 98

Astor, J. J., 72

Babcock, O. E., 45–46

Bank, U. S., Jefferson opposed to, 7; as political issue, 10–11

Beecher, H. W., 78

Belknap, W. W., Secretary of War, 46–47

Bell, John, 14

Belmont, August, 81

Borie, A. E., Secretary of Navy, 39–40

Breckinridge, J. C., 13

Bristow, B. H., Secretary of Treasury, 45

Brooks, James, of N. Y., 44

Bryce, James, quoted, 144

Buchanan, James, continues spoils system, 185

Buckley, "Blind Boss," of San Francisco, 107

Burns, W. J., 110

Burr, Aaron, 65, 66, 87

Butler, B. F., Attorney-General, 31

Butler, E. R., Boss in St. Louis, 102.

Calhoun, J. C., 13

California enacts law to protect primaries (1866), 170

Cameron, Simon, of Penn., 40, 41, 128–30

Campaign committees, 26, 165–167

Campbell, Tom, Republican leader in Cincinnati, 103

Cannon, J. G., Speaker of the House, 144–45

Cass, Lewis, 17

Caucus, The, 20–22

Chandler, Zachariah, 41

Chicago, Municipal Voters' League, 176–77

Cincinnati, Republican, 103; machine rule in, 103–05; partial reform, 105–06

197

AN OUTLINE OF THE PLAN OF
THE CHRONICLES OF AMERICA

The fifty titles of the Series fall into eight topical sequences or groups, each with a dominant theme of its own—

I. *The Morning of America*
TIME: 1492-1763

THE theme of the first sequence is the struggle of nations for the possession of the New World. The mariners of four European kingdoms—Spain, Portugal, France, and England—are intent upon the discovery of a new route to Asia. They come upon the American continent which blocks the way. Spain plants colonies in the south, lured by gold. France, in pursuit of the fur trade, plants colonies in the north. Englishmen, in search of homes and of a wider freedom, occupy the Atlantic seaboard. These Englishmen come in time to need the land into which the French have penetrated by way of the St. Lawrence and the Great Lakes, and a mighty struggle between the two nations takes place in the wilderness, ending in the expulsion of the French. This sequence comprises ten volumes:

1. THE RED MAN'S CONTINENT, *by Ellsworth Huntington*
2. THE SPANISH CONQUERORS, *by Irving Berdine Richman*
3. ELIZABETHAN SEA-DOGS, *by William Wood*
4. CRUSADERS OF NEW FRANCE, *by William Bennett Munro*
5. PIONEERS OF THE OLD SOUTH, *by Mary Johnston*
6. THE FATHERS OF NEW ENGLAND, *by Charles M. Andrews*
7. DUTCH AND ENGLISH ON THE HUDSON, *by Maud Wilder Goodwin*
8. THE QUAKER COLONIES, *by Sydney G. Fisher*
9. COLONIAL FOLKWAYS, *by Charles M. Andrews*
10. THE CONQUEST OF NEW FRANCE, *by George M. Wrong*

II. *The Winning of Independence*
TIME: 1763-1815

The French peril has passed, and the great territory between the Alleghanies and the Mississippi is now open to the Englishmen on the seaboard, with no enemy to contest their right of way except the Indian. But the question arises whether these Englishmen in the New World shall submit to political dictation from the King and Parliament of England. To decide this question the War of the Revolution is fought; the Union is born: and the second war with England follows. Seven volumes:

11. THE EVE OF THE REVOLUTION, *by Carl Becker*
12. WASHINGTON AND HIS COMRADES IN ARMS, *by George M. Wrong*
13. THE FATHERS OF THE CONSTITUTION, *by Max Farrand*
14. WASHINGTON AND HIS COLLEAGUES, *by Henry Jones Ford*
15. JEFFERSON AND HIS COLLEAGUES, *by Allen Johnson*
16. JOHN MARSHALL AND THE CONSTITUTION, *by Edward S. Corwin*
17. THE FIGHT FOR A FREE SEA, *by Ralph D. Paine*

III. *The Vision of the West*
TIME: 1750-1890

The theme of the third sequence is the American frontier—the conquest of the continent from the Alleghanies to the Pacific Ocean. The story covers nearly a century and a half, from the first crossing of the Alleghanies by the backwoodsmen of Pennsylvania, Virginia, and the Carolinas (about 1750) to the heyday of the cowboy on the Great Plains in the latter part of the nineteenth century. This is the marvelous tale of the greatest migrations in history, told in nine volumes as follows:

18. PIONEERS OF THE OLD SOUTHWEST, *by Constance Lindsay Skinner*
19. THE OLD NORTHWEST, *by Frederic Austin Ogg*
20. THE REIGN OF ANDREW JACKSON, *by Frederic Austin Ogg*
21. THE PATHS OF INLAND COMMERCE, *by Archer B. Hulbert*
22. ADVENTURERS OF OREGON, *by Constance Lindsay Skinner*
23. THE SPANISH BORDERLANDS, *by Herbert E. Bolton*
24. TEXAS AND THE MEXICAN WAR, *by Nathaniel W. Stephenson*
25. THE FORTY-NINERS, *by Stewart Edward White*
26. THE PASSING OF THE FRONTIER, *by Emerson Hough*

IV. *The Storm of Secession*

TIME: 1830–1876

The curtain rises on the gathering storm of secession. The theme of the fourth sequence is the preservation of the Union, which carries with it the extermination of slavery. Six volumes as follows:

V. *The Intellectual Life*

Two volumes follow on the higher national life, telling of the nation's great teachers and interpreters:

VI. *The Epic of Commerce and Industry*

The sixth sequence is devoted to the romance of industry and business, and the dominant theme is the transformation caused by the inflow of immigrants and the development and utilization of mechanics on a great scale. The long age of muscular power has passed, and the era of mechanical power has brought with it a new kind of civilization. Eight volumes:

VII. *The Era of World Power*

The seventh sequence carries on the story of government and diplomacy and political expansion from the Reconstruction (1876) to the present day, in six volumes:

VIII. *Our Neighbors*

Now to round out the story of the continent, the Hispanic peoples on the south and the Canadians on the north are taken up where they were dropped further back in the Series, and these peoples are followed down to the present day:

The Chronicles of America is thus a great synthesis, giving a new projection and a new interpretation of American History. These narratives are works of real scholarship, for every one is written after an exhaustive examination of the sources. Many of them contain new facts; some of them —such as those by Howland, Seymour, and Hough—are founded on intimate personal knowledge. But the originality of the Series lies, not chiefly in new facts, but rather in new ideas and new combinations of old facts.

The General Editor of the Series is Dr. Allen Johnson, Chairman of the Department of History of Yale University, and the entire work has been planned, prepared, and published under the control of the Council's Committee on Publications of Yale University.

YALE UNIVERSITY PRESS
143 ELM STREET, NEW HAVEN
522 FIFTH AVENUE, NEW YORK